The Study of the Bible

The Study of the Bible

By

ERNEST CADMAN COLWELL

REVISED EDITION

THE UNIVERSITY OF CHICAGO PRESS

CHICAGO & LONDON

Library of Congress Catalog Card Number: 64-23411

The University of Chicago Press, Chicago & London
The University of Toronto Press, Toronto 5, Canada

*Copyright 1937, 1964 by The University of Chicago. All
rights reserved. Published 1937. Revised Edition 1964
Composed and printed by* THE UNIVERSITY OF CHICAGO
PRESS, *Chicago, Illinois, U.S.A.*

Dedicated in love and esteem
to my parents

ANNA CATHERINE COLWELL
and
ERNEST COLWELL

Preface to the Revised Edition

✻

THIS edition tries to bridge the gap of more than a quarter of a century between the first edition and the present. It does this in two ways: by supplementing the bibliographies and by adding a supplementary chapter.

The bibliographies to chapters i–iii have been completely rewritten. The bibliographies to chapters iv–vi have not been touched, but the reader's attention is called to the bibliography to the new chapter, chapter vii, where recent titles appropriate to these chapters have been added.

In chapter vii the major trends in biblical interpretation in the last thirty years are described. In addition, brief summaries of manuscript discoveries are included.

The author hopes that this book, which found a continuing demand in the last generation, may in this new form serve the present age.

ERNEST CADMAN COLWELL

CLAREMONT, CALIFORNIA
Easter 1964

Preface to the First Edition

✿

A VOLUME that travels through as wide a field as the study of the Bible today soon takes the specialist beyond all the old familiar landmarks out into strange and bewildering territory. In this situation his only hope lies in obtaining local guides who will not suffer his feet to stumble into a crevasse hidden from him by his ignorance. To the many who have tried to keep the author's feet upon the straight and narrow path, he here makes grateful acknowledgment.

Most of all he is indebted to his colleague, Professor William A. Irwin, who read the manuscript in more than one of its stages and made numerous suggestions which have greatly increased its value, especially in the Old Testament area. He did this with characteristic unselfishness at a time when he was heavily burdened with other work. If the book meets the need it was designed to serve, a large part of the credit for its success must go to Mr. Irwin.

Thanks are due also to Professor S. J. Case, Dean of the Divinity School, who read and criticized one of the recensions of the manuscript; to my colleagues in the New Testament Department—Professor H. R. Willoughby, who read the first two chapters, and Professor D. W. Riddle, who made valuable sugges-

tions for the section on interpretation—and to Mr.
B. LeRoy Burkhart, Fellow in the Divinity School of
the University of Chicago, whose patient, accurate,
and stimulating assistance is deeply appreciated. In
the field of linguistic study the author has long been
indebted to Professor J. M. Steadman of Emory University; the chapter on translation owes much to his
teaching.

No one of these scholars is to be held responsible
for the positions taken by the author or for any of the
errors in this work.

The International Council of Religious Education,
owner of the copyright, kindly gave permission for
the use of the American Standard Version of Matt.
3:7–10; Luke 3:7–9; Matt. 9:14–17; Mark 2:18–22;
Luke 5:33–39. This version is published by Thomas
Nelson and Sons, New York City.

ERNEST CADMAN COLWELL

UNIVERSITY OF CHICAGO
February 19, 1937

Introduction

✣

THIS book is an introduction to the study of the Bible, and its primary concern is to prepare the student for his own study of the Bible rather than to present him with an encyclopedic survey of the factual data that have accumulated in the critical investigation of the Christian Scriptures. It is designed to orient the reader in the field of biblical study—to give him a sense of direction, some indication of possible itineraries, a road map with good roads plainly labeled and dangers clearly marked.

It is not planned to minister to the devotional use of the Bible. The author believes that the Bible has valuable contributions to make to modern life, but to define those values here might easily lead to the dogmatic presentation of the author's personal opinion or to a long survey of the many positions taken by others. Neither of these programs falls naturally into the purpose of this book. It gladly recognizes the existence of these values, the need for their study, and the validity of the use of the Bible in modern religious life. But the road it follows leads the student away from these areas toward an intelligent comprehension of what his own Bible is and an introduction to its study.

To this end it presents the problems faced and the resources used in the study of the Bible's origin, transmission, translation, and interpretation. In each of these areas an attempt is made to define the task that faces the student, to describe the helps and hindrances, to explain methods, and to suggest the amount of progress already made. There is no attempt to discuss in comprehensive fashion all the literary or historical problems involved in the study of each of the sixty-six books of the Bible. No attempt is made to survey in detail the history of the canon, or the materials and methods of textual criticism, or to present in summary all that is known in any area of biblical study.

The student who is anxious to go on from this book to such study will find a bibliography at the end of each chapter, which is designed to lead him as far in the pursuit of the subject as his own interest will carry him. The bibliographies group the books referred to under two headings—"General" and "Advanced"—and most of the books listed are briefly characterized. A strenuous effort has been made to include in each of these divisions the clearest and soundest work of contemporary scholarship, preference being given to works which themselves contain good bibliographies and are of recent vintage. A final Bibliography lists periodicals, dictionaries, encyclopedias, series of commentaries, etc.

An especial emphasis is laid upon the part played by the religious experience of the group in the creation of the literature and also upon the part played by the needs of the community in molding the literature into its present form. This is one of the vital interests of biblical scholarship today; and, as it has only recently won prominence, many of the older handbooks give it but scant attention.

This book has been planned to serve as an orientation in the study of the Bible both for those who plan to specialize in the pursuit of biblical lore and also for those whose interest in the subject is of a more general character. The work of many a sincere student is fruitless because his attitudes are basically wrong or his methods unsound. This is often true of the "nonprofessional" student, the undergraduate in college, or the intelligent layman. The questions that come from these sources to the specialist's desk betray a dismaying vulnerability to the attacks of quackery and fanaticism. While no one book can equip the beginner with attitudes and methods adequate for all his needs, this one—it is hoped—will help him toward that attainment. In so far as it accomplishes this it will provide the student with some solid ground on which to stand while he works; it will set up compass marks to prevent his being lost in the confusion of innumerable details and conflicting methods and theories.

Table of Contents

✿

Chapter I
The Origin and Growth of the Bible

✼

THE study of the origin of the Bible begins
with definitions. The Bible, according to a
contemporary dictionary, is the collection of
books which Christians accept as divinely inspired
and as possessing divine authority. Of these two elements—inspiration and authority—it is authority
which is the more distinctive of the Bible. The Bible
is Bible as an authoritative book; any separate book
became Bible when its inspiration was recognized as
of such a quality as to give it authority. The study
of the origin and development of the Bible as Bible
is therefore limited to the study of books accepted as
inspired and authoritative.

DISTINCTION BETWEEN LITERATURE AND CANON

It is equally legitimate to study the books of the
Bible as books. This study of the literature tries to
answer such questions as: Who was the author of the
book? When was it written? Where was it written?
What sources did the author use? etc. Such questions
reach back beyond the existence of the books as Bible
to the time when they existed simply as religious
books. The discussion of this literary criticism of the

Bible is postponed until the origin of the acceptance of the books as authoritative has been investigated. In technical jargon the study of the literary problems of the Bible is called "Introduction"—short for "Introduction to Biblical Literature"—and the study of the Bible as authoritative is called the "study of the canon." It is this canonization of the Scriptures that is studied in this chapter.

The word "canon" is used with a bewildering variety of meanings. It may refer to a support for bells, a bone in a horse's foreleg, a cathedral official, an ecclesiastical law, etc. In terms of Bible study it usually indicates the books accepted as authoritative by the church; that is, it is used as a loose synonym for Bible. But it has other meanings here also. It is used to mean a list of the sacred books; e.g., the Muratorian canon is a Roman list of books accepted by the church about A.D. 180. It is used also of a group of books within the Bible; the manuals speak of "the prophetic canon," "the gospel canon," etc. And in a very broad sense the word "canon" is used to cover the study of the origin and growth of the Bible as Bible; here it is really shorthand for canonization.

Before the student is equipped to face the basic problems involved in a study of how the books of the Bible became sacred, he must assimilate the fact that the literature existed before it was canonized. The existence of the books as nonsacred through a period preceding their acceptance by the cult as authoritative literature has important implications for the study of the canon. It makes impossible the simple assumption that the Jewish people (or the Christian church) rushed to read and obey each new volume before the ink was dry.

We who were born into a church which has reverenced the Scriptures for centuries find it hard to lay aside this casual acceptance of the Bible and see the problems that exist. There have been four gospels in the New Testament since we first saw it—but why four? why not three? or five? or, better yet, why not one? Why two testaments? Why didn't the Christians expand the Jewish Scriptures instead of adding a new volume? How could the Christian church exist for a century without a distinctive Christian canon? Why do the Roman Catholic and the Protestant Old Testaments differ in contents? When and why was the Old Testament Apocrypha dropped from the printings of the English Bible? Has the church ever limited inspiration to the Bible and refused to recognize it elsewhere? These questions are examples of the basic and baffling problems that face the student of the canon. They show clearly that the student must be constantly alert to overcome his familiarity with the Bible, to recognize problems when he meets them, and to travel back into the past—back of the days when there was a Bible.

Most of the Bible was not written as Bible, nor did its first readers read it as Bible. When Paul wrote to his churches, he was so far from expecting that his letters would be accepted as equal in authority to the Jewish Scriptures that he sometimes despaired of hav-

ing his wishes carried out. After writing a harsh letter
to the Corinthians, he worries so much over how it
will be received that he cannot rest but starts toward Corinth to meet his messenger as soon as possible and learn the fate of his letter. When he writes
to Philemon about his slave Onesimus, he bolsters
up this appeal by referring to it in a letter to a church
group. The fiery, almost desperate, tone of his letter
to the Galatian churches springs from the hope but
not from the certainty of converting them to his
position. These are not the attitudes of a man con-
scious of writing sacred scripture and sure of its acceptance as authoritative.

No more dramatic demonstration of the nonsacred
character of these writings in their early form can be
found than the story of the book which Jeremiah
dictated to Baruch to be read before all the people.
As the story is told in chapter 36 of Jeremiah's prophecy, it is plain that some of the leaders of the people
were terrified by what was written in the book; but
the king—the Lord's anointed—was unmoved by its
message, cut it in pieces, and threw it into the fire.
This dramatic rejection is the more interesting in that
the book was a deliberate attempt to influence the
cult group and was written by an individual who held
a recognized position in the life of the cult.

Another instance may be found in the Book of
Amos. The only narrative in this short but vigorous
prophecy relates a stormy interview between the
royal priest and the prophet, in which the prophet
is ordered out of the country. It is quite plain from
this story that there was no overwhelming desire on

the part of king and priest in Israel to accept the message of Amos as divinely authoritative. Somewhere between 750 B.C. and 200 (?) B.C., the Book of Amos acquired authority; and the exact period (if there was any exact period) was certainly closer to the later than the earlier date. Thus, this book must have existed for more than four centuries before it was accepted as part of the authoritative religious literature of the Jewish people.

In the case of those sections of the Bible which had a long preliterary existence, the interval between creation and canonization was even longer. Much of the older material in the Old Testament has a remote past as folklore, poetry, story, and song. For example, it is generally agreed that the major part of the content of the Book of Judges is much older than the book in which we read it. The author, or editor, who compiled our book has such a distinctive and repetitious style that it is easy even for the novice to see the earlier elements within the framework. One of the oldest and most famous of these sections is the Song of Deborah, which may go back to the twelfth century B.C. It is a sweeping, partisan, brutal song of war and victory and exultation over the enemy—a true war song. Our Book of Judges was written toward the end of the fifth century B.C. and was accepted as scripture by 200 (?) B.C. In the seven hundred years that Deborah's Song was sung by Jewish patriots, was it accepted as an authoritative religious guide by the cult as a cult? To ask the question is to answer it with a negative.

Examples of this sort could be multiplied until the

reader was lulled to sleep by their monotony. There are large areas in the Pentateuch whose composition is separated from their acceptance by an interval of many centuries. This is true also of most of the other books of the Old Testament. Sometimes in them we catch glimpses of the literature before our literature. There are quotations from, and references to, other books; e.g., the Book of Jasher is quoted, but no one supposes that Jasher was ever regarded as an authoritative volume in the sense that Genesis later was. Even some of the latest books in the Old Testament —e.g., Chronicles—give evidence of using ancient volumes as sources. The existence of these ancient books behind our biblical books shows how long a pre-biblical history much of the Bible had.

It is clear from even this sampling of the literature that the origin of the canon is not to be found in the study of the origin of the individual books as books. The process we study here is a secondary one. First, the literature is produced, used, edited, collected, re-edited; then, after a longer or a shorter interval of time, it is accepted by the cult as sacred and authoritative—as Bible.

WHY HAVE A BIBLE?

But why? Why was it ever accepted as Bible? This is the basic and most baffling problem in the history of the canon. It must not be lightly assumed that the production and acceptance of a sacred authoritative book is inevitable in every cult simply because it is a cult. It is easy for a religion to exist without a book.

Many religions have so existed; some still do. One of the most vigorous competitors of Christianity in the Roman empire was the cult of the sun god Mithras. It swept through the legions and spread rapidly to the frontiers of the empire, yet it was in no sense a book religion. The answer to the question, "Why have a Bible?" must, therefore, be sought in some of the characteristic features of Jewish religion and life.

The remote distance at which the process of canonization began adds to the difficulty of answering this primal question. The reason for later developments and for the formation of new canons is determined with relative ease; for in these later areas we have, as one influential element in the situation, the presence of the first sacred collection, and the amount of contemporary evidence as to the process increases as the story approaches modern times. It is easy to say why Mohammed produced an authoritative book for his cult, but the activity of pious Jews in the seventh century B.C. follows no well-known precedent and is shrouded in the obscurity of antiquity.

The movement toward the creation of an authoritative religious literature rose out of the conception of the nation as the chosen people of a particular deity. Since this conception was not peculiar to Israel and existed in other nations before the Exodus, the ultimate source of the canon lies in the early history of cultures that were old before the Hebrews came to the promised land. If the nation exists in an intimate reciprocal relationship to the deity, it naturally fol-

lows that the laws of the nation are God's laws and
that the history of the nation is sacred history. Furthermore, the deity would not be so thoughtless of
his people as to cut them off from the prospect of
receiving additional messages from him as occasion
demanded. Throughout the ancient world prophets
appeared who spoke for God, whose words had a
degree of sanctity derived from the source from which
they came. It was, therefore, not only possible but
natural that codes of law, books of history, and sermons of the prophets should attain to some measure
of sanctity.

A concrete representation of this is to be seen on
the Susa stele found in A.D. 1901 and written about
2000 B.C. Here the Babylonian king Hammurabi is
shown in bas-relief, standing on a mountain top before his god, who hands him the laws inscribed be-
neath them. Several of the precepts of this code are
strikingly parallel to items in the Code of the Covenant (Exod. 20:23—23:19); e.g., the demand of an
eye for an eye and the prescriptions as to liability for
damages incurred by the owner of a goring ox. Thus
the code of Hammurabi and the covenant code in
Exodus alike possessed some degree of divine authority from the day of their codification at least. But
their early users were still far from regarding them
as part of a Bible.

CANONS ARE ADOPTED IN CRISES

Some light is shed on the origin of the Bible as Bible
by the study of certain characteristics which are com-

mon to the various specific situations in which formal canonization emerges. One of these common elements is the presence of strife between parties within the cult.

At least from the time when the Hebrew people settled in Canaan, there was conflict between the rigorous religion they brought with them from the desert—which we later call "prophetic"—and the softer cult of the people of the land with their Baalim. The influence of the Canaanite religion upon that of the Hebrews was ancient, strong, and persistent. One of the recent archeological discoveries emphasizes the extent of its influence upon even the early ritual. Our biblical history is written from the prophetic and priestly viewpoint; thus those kings are good who keep the cult "pure," and those are bad who favor and foster Canaanitish elements and practices. One of the worst kings in this regard was Manasseh, who ruled in the first half of the seventh century b.c. He restored and enriched the hillside shrines and favored the Canaanitish elements in the cult. A few years after the death of Manasseh, the prophetic party greatly influenced his grandson, King Josiah.

This influence culminated in the reforms of 621 b.c., which consisted of the abolition of all shrines except the temple in Jerusalem and the adoption of a book found in the temple as a religious authority for the people. This book with its anti-Canaanitish emphasis was written by some leader of the opposition to Manasseh in the dark days before Josiah came to the throne. This explains the rigorous nature of

the legislation—the destruction of all shrines but one.
Josiah's acceptance of the teachings of the party opposed to Amon and Manasseh could not be transferred to the mass of the people as a casual or routine
matter. The ruthless nature of the reversal of policy
and the destruction of all shrines outside Jerusalem
must have stirred the people deeply and unsettled
many. In that time of disquiet the change was supported by a new authority—the adoption of a sacred
book. Scholars identify this book as the core of the
present Book of Deuteronomy.

Another example of the emergence of formal canonization in situations marked by strife within the
cult can be seen in the story of the New Testament
canon in the second century A.D. In this century the
vitality of the new cult was too exuberant to be stereotyped by the elementary controls that the church
possessed at that time. The result was that division
followed division in rapid succession: Docetism,
Gnosticism, the Marcionite schism, Montanism. The
second century has been well called the blossom time
of the sects. The strongest of these sects, or heresies,
was that led by Marcion. About the middle of the
century, he attempted to convert the Ephesian and
then the Roman church to his views. When he failed,
he organized his followers into Marcionite churches.

He bitterly attacked the Old Testament, claiming
that it was not inspired by the Father of Jesus but
by an inferior deity. He claimed to be a true representative of the apostles, especially of Paul (the only
true representative of Jesus); and he supplied his

churches with a New Testament consisting of "Gospel and Apostle" (Luke and Paul) to replace the Old Testament. Thus he set an ancient authority (ancient in Christian history) which had already acquired some prestige over against the authority of local ecclesiastical officials—the bishop and presbyters of Rome and of other cities. Within a generation of his arrival at Rome, the Roman church set up a definite list of books which it accepted as authoritative. This earliest list of New Testament books, called the "Muratorian canon," emerges in a situation characterized by strife within the cult.

CANONS ARE ADOPTED UNDER POLITICAL PRESSURE

A second element common to the various situations in which the formal acceptance of the canon takes place is the presence of pressure upon the cult arising from the association of the cult with political life. This can be seen both in times of disaster and in times of triumph. The classic example from days of disaster is the "closing" of the Old Testament canon in Palestinian Judaism. Jerusalem had been captured by the Romans in the year 70, and the temple ritual abolished by the destruction of the temple. This mortal blow to the existence of the Jewish people in the sacred land raised questions of many kinds in regard to the continuing life of the cult. The leaders of the synagogue faced the trying situation and put forth desperate efforts to establish and strengthen the remaining resources of the cult.

One of the most valuable of these resources was the Sacred Book, which at that time consisted of three collections of books—the Law, the Prophets, and the other writings. The first two were definite in content and accepted beyond question; the third group had no sharpness of outline, and about some books the question of inclusion or omission was a very live one. The weakening of the religion consequent to the disaster of A.D. 70 made this uncertainty as to the exact limits of the Bible intolerable; and the rabbis of Palestine began an intensive discussion of the Bible's contents which led ultimately to agreement on its exact limits.

In the second century B.C. the strenuous efforts of King Antiochus Epiphanes of Syria to stamp out the religion of his Jewish subjects introduced a period of conflict between cult and state of great significance for the canon. The attack was begun before the days of Antiochus, for the attractive features of Hellenism had drawn many Jews away from their loyalty to their own cult. The critical nature of the situation when Antiochus threw the military power of the state against Judaism cannot be overemphasized. Pious Jews did not underestimate the danger; under the military leadership of Judas and his family they repulsed invaders, threw off the Syrian yoke, and attained an approximate independence. Since the Syrian persecution deliberately singled out the sacred books of the Jews for destruction, and even forbade the reading of the Scriptures, it was important to know which books were Scriptures. This situation made a vital issue of the exact definition of the Bible's contents. From it, in all probability, came the impetus to the final definition of the prophetic canon, the second division of the Jewish Bible.

Although we know little of the details of the action, there can be no doubt that Jewish leaders found in their military victories a victory for Torah, too. It is perhaps an oversimplification of the processes to point out that the three great national disasters of Israel —(1) the Babylonian captivity, (2) the Syrian persecution, and (3) the capture of Jerusalem by the Romans—are followed in turn by the closing of the three divisions of the Jewish Bible—(1) the Law (2) the Prophets, and (3) the Writings.

The pressure exerted upon the cult in regard to the formation of the canon by the association of the cult with political life was equally strong in days of triumph. Early in the fourth century A.D., Christianity won tolerance and favor from the Emperor Constantine; and in A.D. 380 Theodosius I proclaimed Christianity the official religion of the state. That Constantine's recognition sprang from a desire to strengthen the unity of the empire is shown by the strenuous efforts he made to bring the dissident groups of the church into harmony. Dislike of heresy (that is, of division) in the dominant cult of the realm has characterized other able rulers since Constantine; Theodosius' denial to heretics of the right to make bequests indicates plainly the value he attached to a united church. That the pressure toward unification which the state brought to bear upon the church throughout the fourth century affected canon as well as doctrine is certain, for the value of canon as a source of doctrine was unquestioned. It is not chance coincidence that this century which saw the church become the one religion of the state saw the church agree on one canon. That this agreement was still far from unanimous is true; it would, perhaps, be more accurate to say that the degree of agreement here reached its high point. The exaltation of the church at the right hand of the emperor takes place in the period which sees the Christian canon formally completed.

WHAT BOOKS ARE TO BE INCLUDED?

The question raised above—Why a Bible?—is partly answered by the fact that in the crucial situations (like those described above) there was at hand a body of literature which had already acquired some prestige.

This prestige was in part due to the antiquity of the literature at the time of its canonization. In the Roman Catholic church today no person is canonized until at least fifty years after the date of death. In the history of the growth of the Bible, the interval between the writing of a book and its canonization was always greater than that—or was believed to be so. The first codes of laws to acquire prestige claim Moses as their author and are written against the birth of the Hebrew people (the Exodus) as a background. In the Christian Testament, literature that went back to Jesus and his circle gained prestige from the tremendous significance of Jesus for the church. From the moment of the resurrection appearances, Jesus loomed so large on the stage of Christian history that the Gospels, for example, from the time they were written possessed importance from the fact that they told about Jesus.

But, in the longer span of Old Testament history especially, the preceding point does not explain how these books came to be preserved long enough to acquire the sanctity of antiquity. The origin of the canon is not explained by quoting the venerable saying about religion's habit of sanctifying everything more than five hundred years old, for the puzzling query still remains, "How did these books acquire enough prestige to attain such an advanced age?"

The sanctity ascribed to a book as Bible was first and most naturally ascribed to cult prescriptions. In Exodus, chapter 34, an ancient code describes the covenant made between Jahweh and Moses and contains a decalogue which is entirely cultic. Its ritual legislation prescribes the feast of unleavened bread, the offering of first-born males (except the first-born of an ass or of man), the Sabbath rest, the feast of weeks, the feast of ingathering at the year's end, the use of unleavened bread, and the offering of the first of the crop. It forbids leaving the sacrifice of the feast of the Passover until the morning and boiling a kid in its mother's milk. It is easily seen that prescriptions and proscriptions of this sort would early acquire a sacred authority from the intimacy of their association with the rites of the cult.

It is no accident that the first code formally accepted by the Jews as Bible (the Deuteronomic code) included laws controlling the location of the temple, the observance of the religious festivals, the paying of tithes, etc. This code itself acquires antiquity and prestige through its ascription to Moses and the quotation of older laws, beginning with the Ten Commandments. Many of its prescriptions are much older than 621 B.C.; Deuteronomy simply transfers the location of their observance from the country shrines to Jerusalem. The transference was due to the contemporary crisis; the prescriptions had already acquired antiquity through the vitality and conservatism of cult practice.

But the services rendered to the cult by religious books were not all of a liturgical nature. Other elements than liturgy survive or recur from generation to generation. The problems met by one individual in his lifetime are not entirely and uniquely his own. Some of the righteous are poor and afflicted in every generation; so many of the good persist in dying young that they have created a proverb. Neither false friends nor scolding wives are modern inventions, nor is the divorce of the wife of one's youth a new device of the shyster lawyer of today. Short weights and measures and the exploitation of labor have ancient precedents. Religious books that championed the good life and tackled these problems interested more than one generation; the cult found enough value in them to keep them alive.

Liturgy and personal morality by no means exhaust

the areas served through successive generations by religious books, but these two are significant examples of the values which won survival for the religious book in its precanonical days. Thus the first answer given to the question, "What books?" is, "A book already ancient, already revered from intimate association with the cult or from the enduring service of recurrent needs, and useful to the dominant element in the cult in days of crisis."

The question, "What books are to be included?" has often been answered too simply by saying, "those books which were read in public worship, whether of synagogue or church." I say "too simply," for there are books in the canon that were not read in the synagogue or the church service. The books of the Writings, or Hagiographa, the third section of the Old Testament canon, were not read in the synagogue service. That is to say, in the formal systems of lections for Sabbath reading throughout the year, no use was made of the Writings; the use of the five rolls in connection with the festivals is hardly analogous. The Revelation of John was not read in church service in early Christian days; the lectionaries of the Orthodox church derive no lections from it. There are Gospel lectionaries and Apostle (Acts and Epistles) lectionaries, but no Apocalypse lectionaries.

Not only are there books in the canon that were not read in church but there are some books that were read in synagogue or church only after they were accepted as canonical. Does anyone imagine that the Deuteronomic code was read in sacred service for a long time and thus became Bible? Of course not. Throughout the entire history of the development of the Jewish Bible it is difficult to establish clearly the chronological order of synagogue reading and canonization.

Moreover, some books were read in church services —and probably also in the synagogue—that never became part of the Bible. At an early point in the development of the liturgy, the stories of the martyrs were read in church service; they are still being read in the appropriate services of the ancient communions; but they are not in the Bible. Nor can any clear case be made for the claim that they ever came near to sanctity. The letter of Clement of Rome to the Corinthians is another instance of widespread and long-continued church reading which did not lead to canonization. Eusebius (*Church History* iii. 16) makes a strong statement as to this use of I Clement: "It has been read publicly before the congregation in very many churches from a long time ago, and [is so read] in our own time."

At least one important book, the Psalter, obtained its place not because it was read in synagogue or church but because it was sung in the temple at Jerusalem. This intimate association with the ritual of the cult gave it a prestige great enough to lead to its inclusion in the Jewish Bible after the Law and the Prophets were closed. It is quite probable that it was the importance of the Psalter that kept the Old Testament canon open after the collection of the Prophets had been completed. It led the way to the

dogma that prophecy was dead. This teaching arose from the closing of the second section of the canon, not from the disappearance of prophets and prophecy in Israel. The writings of Josephus, the New Testament itself, and the Old Testament Apocrypha and Pseudepigrapha with their frequent references to prophets and prophecy, all clearly show that prophecy was still vital in Jewish religion in the first century B.C. and in the first century A.D.

After the closing of the prophetic canon, prophets wrote "prophecies" (apocalypses) in which the author borrows the mantle of some ancient worthy so that his book may reach back of the closing of the prophetic canon into a period when authoritative books of prophecy could still be written. The strong opposition to the inclusion of Daniel sprang from the fact that it won importance as a prophecy after the prophetic canon was closed. It was only when its disguise was accepted at face value that this prophecy was reluctantly included. That is to say, its claims to being an ancient work could only be accepted after the date of its appearance was forgotten, and it had to be accepted as ancient before it was accepted as prophetic.

The argument over whether or not a disputed book of the Writings is "prophetic" is thus seen to rest on the determination of date. The same thing is true in the use of the term "apostolic" in New Testament controversy. For better or for worse, the sec ond century A.D. saw the Christian churches accepting apostolicity as the test of a book's right to a place in the canon. But to be apostolic a book had to be (relatively) old. Thus the Muratorian list (A.D. 180–200) rejects the Shepherd of Hermas, an apocalypse (prophecy). The reasons given are that it was written quite recently, "in our own times"; that it cannot be included with the Prophets, whose number is complete, or with the apostolic group since Hermas has just appeared.

How were groups of books collected, and the collection closed? The collecting began as a natural, that is, a spontaneous, movement; it ended in some formal authoritative action. For example, there can be little doubt that the captivity in Babylon led to a new appreciation of the message of Jeremiah. In a sense the destruction of Jerusalem and the exile confirmed his preaching. From the reading of Jeremiah to the reading of other prophets of doom was a natural and easy step. The collection grew slowly and irregularly from the exile to the second century B.C., as the Jewish people found inspiration and encouragement in the writings of these vigorous preachers of righteousness. The closing of this particular collection is shrouded in obscurity. The explanation often heard that the dying-out of prophecy finally led to the acceptance of these surviving prophetic books will not bear careful scrutiny, as we have shown above. A more probable situation for the formal closing of the prophetic canon existed in the Maccabean period after Antiochus' attack on the Scripture had been beaten back.

In the absence of direct evidence it is dangerous to speculate on the action that closed the prophetic canon. Yet it seems clear that it was closed not only out of reverence for the old prophets but also out of fear and dislike of the new ones. The post-Exilic period is one in which the priest and the scribe attain an ever increasing importance in the cult; they are themselves officialized and institutionalized—the one in connection with the temple; the other, with the synagogue. That their leaders came to depreciate contemporary prophecy, always inclining toward independence of established authority, was natural. That had happened in the days of Amos; it happened in Jesus' day; it probably happened in Jerusalem in the Ptolemaic period. The fanatical extravagance and independence of some "prophets" in the late third century B.C., or in the turbulent days of the Maccabees, was probably part of the cause of the official closing of the prophetic canon; and the closing was probably made official by the willing co-operation of the priesthood.

Toward the end of the second century A.D. the Christian church went through a similar experience. The Montanist movement placed a high value on spirit guidance and prophecy. These prophets set their direct inspiration over against the prestige slowly built up by local bishops and by earlier writings. That the officials of the church in this situation referred to the closed nature of the prophetic canon was natural; that they used the growing prestige of the apostles to shut out these books was equally natural; and in the Muratorian canon's treatment of the Prophecy of Hermas we have an example of this exclusion in action. Ultimately, all prophecies but one were excluded from the New Testament; the inclusion of that one was due to its claim of apostolic authorship. This ultimate canon was, of course, a canon promulgated by councils and ecclesiastics. This was true also—as we have already noted—of the closing of the canon of the Writings in the Old Testament, closed for Palestinian Jews by the pronouncements of rabbis. The first canonical book was officially accepted by the people under the leadership of king and priest. All later books canonized came to their final acceptance in a closed collection through some official action. Yet the official action, generally speaking, is no more than the ratification of a popular choice manifested by the continuing use of the books in the private devotions of the individual as well as in cult usage. Let this fact be emphasized as it deserves (and it is the most important validation of the canon to the modern man), it must still be remembered that the acceptance of the same list of books by the vast majority of the membership of a cult is historically incredible without some formal authorization.

The books chosen were not always the same; in fact, a brief survey of any elementary introduction to the canon leaves one with the impression that they were never the same. The amount of this variation may be indicated by the extreme and yet accurate statement that exactly the same Bible (as to books included) was never accepted at any one time by all the believers in the cult. The church member today is aware that there is some sort of difference in content between Roman Catholic and Protestant Bibles; the student in college and seminary has a faint and accurate idea that there was an equal difference in the contents of the Jewish canon as it existed for the Jew of Palestine and the Jew of Alexandria in A.D. 30. It is not our purpose here to list all the known differences in Bibles' contents—the lists can be easily found in the books referred to in the bibliography—but rather to raise as sharply as possible a question as to the reason for this variation and to suggest some of the possible answers.

Sometimes the difference in canonical lists is due to what may be called "historical accident." Under this none-too-satisfactory heading various incidents and influences may be grouped; the discussion of examples will make the meaning of the term clearer than a wordy definition could hope to do.

The Samaritans pride themselves on being the true Israel; their Sacred Scripture contains the Pentateuch and nothing else. The present tense is used in speaking of them because they still exist (although in dwindling numbers) as a distinct sect in Palestine. The division between Jews and Samaritans became final and irreconcilable in the days of Alexander the Great. The Pentateuch had been formally accepted by the Jewish people about a generation earlier; the Samaritans, therefore, naturally carried the Scripture with them in their separation from the Jews of Jerusalem. The propinquity and similarities between these two rival cults generated such bitterness that any transfer of sacred books adopted by the Jews after the split was an impossibility. Ill will began between the groups in Samaritan opposition to Jewish innovations, although the Jewish leaders regarded their work as reform and return to older patterns. This conservatism prevented the growth of the Samaritan canon; but, had the schism been delayed a century and a half, the Samaritan canon would consist of the Law and the Prophets.

Another example of the influence of "historical accidents" upon the process of canonization can be seen in the case of the Book of Esther. Esther was read in connection with the feast of Purim by the Jews of the Dispersion within a short time of its composition. But the Palestinian Jews celebrated as an important religious festival Judas Maccabaeus' victory over Nicanor on the very day on which the Jews of the Dispersion first celebrated the feast of Purim. Consequently, this feast (Purim) did not enter Palestine until some centuries after its establishment. As a secondary consequence, since Esther gained religious prestige from being read in connection with the observance of Purim, Esther was accepted as canonical much sooner outside Palestine than inside Palestine. But, if Judas had attacked Nicanor a day or a week sooner. . . . .

Differences in content sprang also from the absence of a critical situation and consequent formal canonization in one part of the world and its presence in another section. We have already seen that the Jewish war and the destruction of Jerusalem in A.D. 70 were influential in leading to the closing of the scriptural canon in Palestine. But there was in the Dispersion no analogous crisis involving the Bible, and as a result the canon was not formally closed in the Dispersion at this time. Hence the extra-Palestinian Bible contained from eight to a dozen books not in the Scriptures accepted in the Holy Land.

We have seen that the irritating influence of Marcion and his creation of a New Testament at Rome did much to make the Roman church aware of the need of an authoritative pronouncement on the Bible. It was in large measure the presence of this aggressive and capable schismatic that made Rome conservative on the matter of the contents of the Bible. How would the story of the canon read today if Marcion had gone to the city of Alexandria instead of to Rome?

There was also a difference in the rate at which books were accepted as authoritative by the churches in the important cities, on the one hand, and the churches of the backwoods districts, the hinterland, on the other. The big cities were often in closer touch with one another than they were with the small churches scattered through the adjacent rural sections. One could travel easily and rapidly from city to city—especially the cities on or near the Mediterranean Sea. In the big cities local judgment was easily influenced by the decisions made in other important churches; thus their canons at least kept within sight of one another. But in the backwoods the small amount of intercommunication left the local or sectional church more independent in its choice. As a result, the churches of these areas either lagged behind the majority in accepting new books as canon (as was the case in Syria outside Antioch) or continued to accept books unchecked by outside criticism (as was the case in Ethiopia and, to some extent, in Armenia).

These facts may be covered by the generalization that some areas were more cautious or conservative in the matter of canonization than others. The outlying districts of Syria were more conservative than Antioch; Palestinian Judaism than the Diaspora; Rome than Alexandria.

The conservatism of the Syrian territory is seen in both Old Testament and New Testament. Its Old Testament did not include Chronicles; through the fourth century its New Testament included neither Catholic Epistles nor Apocalypse. But, as Chrysostom's usage shows, the city of Antioch had already accepted three of the Catholic letters: James, I Peter, and I John.

This conservatism of Syria was in accord with the conservatism of Palestine in regard to the Old Testament canon. The canon as adopted in Palestine toward the end of the first century was identical with that of the present-day Protestant Old Testament. At that time there was still some hesitation as to the acceptance of even some of these books—Esther, Ezra-Nehemiah, Chronicles, and the Song of Songs. Jews outside of Palestine were much freer in their treatment of the canon, which they used in the Greek translation called the Septuagint. They accepted books more rapidly than the Palestinians; they amplified some of the books they both accepted; they were evidently less concerned about the limits of the canon than were their compatriots in the homeland. Thus we cannot be too confident that every book found in a manuscript of the Septuagint was an integral part of the Bible for Alexandrian Jews. But the evidence is sufficient to indicate a much larger canon at Alexandria than was accepted in Jerusalem. Among the books they received are the following: I and II Esdras, Tobit, Judith, Additions to Esther, Wisdom of Solomon, Wisdom of Jesus the son of Sirach (Ecclesiasticus), Baruch, Additions to Daniel, Prayer of Manasses, I–II Maccabees. Of these, only Ecclesiasticus enjoyed any prestige in Palestine.

In the Christian church of Alexandria an equally liberal view as to the contents of Scripture was dominant. In the writings of Clement we see the same inclusive and carefree attitude toward Christian Scripture that we have noticed in the Jews of Alexandria toward the Old Testament. Clement used half-a-dozen gospels; fourteen letters of Paul; six Catholic epistles—including Barnabas and I Clement; three Apocalypses—John, Peter, and Hermas—the Acts of the Apostles; the Preaching of Peter; and the Didache. Except for his surplus gospels, most of these works are either explicitly or implicitly used as Scripture by Clement. Thus Alexandria was the home of an extensive Scripture in both Testaments. It is no

accident that it was also the home of allegorical interpretation. The use of this method of interpretation—
from pre-Christian times on—made it possible for the
Alexandrian to overcome difficulties in regard to
canonical books very easily. In Palestine and Syria
a more sedate, more literal and historical criticism
was employed. This goes far toward explaining the
variations in canon in the two sections.

Rome was early forced by Marcion into the defini-
tion of the Scriptures. Its New Testament never
knew the exuberance of the Alexandrian, but its Old
Testament grew into practical identity with that of
Egypt. In the Christian books the affinities of Rome
are—in general—with Syria and Asia Minor; in the
Jewish Scriptures it reaches through North Africa to
Alexandria and a "full" Old Testament.

The student who faces the problems raised by these
variations in the contents of the Bible can simplify
his task by establishing a list of those books commonly accepted throughout the cult. In the Old Testament these unquestioned books include the Protestant Old Testament with the exception of Esther,
Ezra-Nehemiah, Chronicles, Daniel, Song of Solomon, and—perhaps—Job and Ecclesiastes. In the
New Testament the unquestioned books are the Four
Gospels, the Acts, and ten letters of Paul. The books
which won their place in the final official canon only
after the dissent of a minority had been overcome
are the crucial points for study in the history of the
canonization of individual books. The pronouncements of councils did more for these "disputed" books
than for the rest of the Bible.

What these councils really ratified for these disputed books was their authenticity in terms of author and date. It was in the final period of canon formation that questions as to authorship played their supremely important part. If the letter to the Hebrews was the work of Paul, then it was apostolic and deserved a place in the Christian canon. It is doubtful if questions of authorship have had any vital importance for the Scriptures in any other period. Nor has any more artificial method of determining authorship been employed than the majority vote of a council of ecclesiastics. If these councils had made fewer mistakes, the work of modern scholarship would be much less "negative."

AFTER THE LAST COUNCIL

The minor role played by decisions of councils is shown by the precarious existence of those books which owed their position in the canon largely to the favorable verdict of some council. Not all books in the canon—even if they had been formally and officially accredited—were received by the faithful with the same degree of reverence and enthusiasm. The books which enjoyed the most prestige were those whose canonization was merely a recognition of general and long-established usage.

Thus, in the Hebrew Scriptures, no later book or books ever attained to the pre-eminence occupied by the Law. Within the Holy Book, the Law was the Holy of Holies. Next to it in general esteem came the Prophets, but the Prophets were definitely below the Law in sanctity. This is most dramatically shown in the prescriptions for the reading of the Bible in synagogue services. In New Testament times it was customary to read from the Hebrew in short passages which were translated at once into Aramaic by the Meturgeman so that the Scripture might be understood by the congregation that knew no Hebrew. The rule as given in the Mishna (*Megilla* iv. 4) follows: "He who reads in the Pentateuch must not read to the Meturgeman more than one verse, and in the Prophets three verses [at a time]. If each verse is a paragraph, they are read one by one. He who reads may skip in the Prophets, but not in the Law." Equally significant as to the relative prestige of the various sections of the canon is the fact that the Writings—the third section of the Old Testament— was not read at all in synagogue services.

What Torah was to the Jew, the Gospel was to the Christian. Its pre-eminence is shown not only by its appearance in every Christian canon but also by the favor shown it by the members of the cult. This can be seen objectively in the number of manuscripts of the Greek New Testament in existence today. Manuscripts of the Four Gospels number more than two thousand; in addition, there are more than a thousand Gospel lectionary manuscripts. Manuscripts of the Acts and Epistles and their lectionary are less than half as numerous. There are less than two hundred manuscripts of Revelation, aside from fragments. These totals accurately represent the relative prestige of these volumes in Eastern Christendom down through the Middle Ages.

No decree of a council could ever give to any Christian book the prestige enjoyed by the Gospel. No council of rabbis could ever lift any other volume to the level of Torah. Nor did formal acceptance by the leaders of the cult always mean vital acceptance by the mass of the believers. It is sometimes said that the Jewish canon was closed in Palestine about A.D. 90 with the acceptance of Esther, Song of Solomon, Daniel, Ezra-Nehemiah, and Chronicles. Yet the Syriac version—dominated by Palestinian ideals— did not include Chronicles. Esther was not accepted by Theodore of Mopsuestia; by the Nestorians; by the Palestinians whom Melito visited about A.D. 150; by Athanasius of Alexandria in A.D. 365; by Gregory Nazianzen (†A.D. 389). The Talmud itself contains items that show Esther was not universally accepted after A.D. 100. The Babylonian Gemara (fol. 7a) of the tractate *Megilla* tries to meet the difficulties caused by Rabbi Samuel's statement that Esther was not canonical. The tractate *Sanhedrin* (fol. 100a) states that Esther does not need covers as canonical books do. It was only the association of Esther with the feast of Purim that gradually increased its prestige. In the Christian church, in periods of freedom of thought, Esther has once more been under attack. Luther, in speaking of II Maccabees, said: "I am so opposed to this book and to Esther that I wish they did not exist, for they Judaize too much, and have many heathenish improprieties." So far is the pious layman today from using his Bible as equally valuable in all its parts that he is willing to award

some badge of merit to anyone who has read the
Bible all the way through; he, himself, very naturally
and justifiably, selects his readings from those areas
which he finds most inspiring.

What we have seen to be true in the case of Esther
was equally true in the experience of the Apocalypse
of John in the New Testament canon. It was not
popular in the Eastern half of the Roman world; Con-
stantinople, Antioch, Syria, and Caesarea were not
enthusiastic about it as part of the canon. Yet, under
the wing of Rome, Africa, and Alexandria, it was
formally declared canonical at Hippo and Carthage
in councils at the end of the fourth century, by
Athanasius of Alexandria (A.D. 367), by Basil the
Great (†A.D. 379), and by Gregory of Nyssa (†*ca.* A.D.
394), as by many others. In the West it first appeared in the Muratorian canon (*ca.* 180) and was an
integral part of the canon throughout the Middle
Ages. But in the East its position was never secure.
Two of the four Doctors of the Orthodox church
(Chrysostom and Gregory of Nazianzus) did not accept Revelation as canonical. It was not in the Old
Syriac version or in the Syriac Peshitta (*ca.* 425). It
was not in the original Armenian version. Theodore
of Mopsuestia (†A.D. 428), Amphilochius of Iconium
(†A.D. 394), the sixtieth canon of "Laodicea," the List
of the Sixty Canonical Books, all reject the Apocalypse. Even as late as A.D. 850, it is listed as a "disputed" book in the Stichometry of Nicephorus.

In spite of formal canonization, the Revelation of
John did not win widespread acceptance in the East.

We have already noticed that in number of manuscripts extant its total is about one-seventh of that of manuscripts of the Gospels. Moreover, many of these manuscripts are not part of larger New Testaments but often contain noncanonical material. Nor did the Orthodox church use the Book of Revelation in its preparation of lections for use in the liturgy; to this day it is not read regularly in church services.

An unusual example of the lower level of canonicity enjoyed by the Apocalypse was noted in the study of a sixteenth-century Greek manuscript containing the Apocalypse and commentary, translated into conversational Greek of the period. In the comment other books of the Bible are quoted, but it is the author's general rule not to translate them into the conversational idiom—they were too sacred! Yet the main purpose of this work was to translate the Apocalypse into conversational idiom.

In the Western world Luther's opinion of the Apocalypse is well known; less familiar is the similar judgment of the Roman Catholic scholar Erasmus (expressed at the end of his notes on the first edition of the Greek New Testament). He comments on its vicissitudes in the past with keen discernment, raises questions as to its authorship, and concludes with an analogy whose accuracy cannot be concealed even by the decision of an ecumenical council. "Since even among jewels," he says, "there is some difference, and some gold is purer and better than other; in sacred things also one thing is more sacred than another."

This discussion of the origin and growth of the

Bible is designed to open up the field for study. It raises questions as to the ultimate origin of the canon and tries to indicate its process of growth. The part played by heresy and council in advancing the canon has been suggested with no attempt at comprehensive treatment. The important Council of Trent, for example, has been passed over in silence. For the pursuit of factual material, and a study of other problems, the student's attention is called to the bibliography that follows.

BIBLIOGRAPHY ON CANON

GENERAL

PFEIFFER, R. H., "The Canon of the Old Testament," and BEARE, F. W., "The Canon of the New Testament," in *The Interpreter's Dictionary of the Bible*. Nashville: Abingdon, 1962.

JEFFERY, A., "The Canon of the Old Testament," and GOODSPEED, E. J., "The Canon of the New Testament," in *The Interpreter's Bible*, Vol. I. Nashville: Abingdon, 1952.

ADVANCED

In Introductions to the Literature; e.g.,

WIKENHAUSER, A. *New Testament Introduction* (trans. by JOSEPH CUNNINGHAM). New York: Herder & Herder, 1960.
Part I deals with the canon of the New Testament. Good bibliography.

WEISER, ARTUR. *The Old Testament: Its Formation and Development*. New York: Association Press, 1961.
Second part deals with canon.

SOUTER, A. *The Text and Canon of the New Testament* (2d ed. revised by C. S. C. WILLIAMS). London: Duckworth, 1953.

FILSON, F. V. *Which Books Belong in the Bible: A Study of the Canon.* Philadelphia: Westminster, 1957.

A discussion of the theological issues involved in canonization.

ÖSTBARN, GUNNAR. *Cult and Canon.* (No. 10 in Uppsala Universitets Arsskift, Acta Universitatis Upsaliensis.) Uppsala: A.-B. Lundequistska Bokhandeln, 1950.

ZEITLIN, S. *An Historical Study of the Canonization of the Hebrew Scriptures.* (Offprint from the *Proceedings of the American Academy for Jewish Research, 1931–1932.*) Philadelphia: Jewish Publication Society, 1933.

An independent and stimulating study which makes large use of rabbinic sources and reaches some conclusions at variance with those generally received.

ENSLIN, MORTON S. *Christian Beginnings*, pp. 455–74: "On the Way to a Canon." New York: Harper & Bros., 1938.

Brief but stimulating survey of the origin of the New Testament canon.

HARNACK, ADOLF VON. *The Origin of the New Testament* (trans. by J. R. WILKINSON). New York: Macmillan, 1925.

The most stimulating definition of the problems involved in the making of the New Testament canon.

WESTCOTT, B. F. *A General Survey of the History of the Canon of the New Testament* (7th ed.). New York: Macmillan, 1896.

A full presentation of the relevant data; most of the important sources are quoted in the original language. Useful as a reference work.

Chapter II
The Transmission of the Bible

✿

THE letters Paul wrote have all vanished. We have none of the autographs, the originals, of the books of the Bible. The exact transcript as it came from the author's pen has disappeared. It is generally believed now that these originals vanished fairly soon after they were written. The New Testament books probably had a shorter life than those of the Jewish Scriptures, for they were most probably written on perishable papyrus, while the books of the Old Covenant may have been written on skins—a much more durable material. In the loss of the original manuscripts, the Bible is on a par with most of the literary works of antiquity; for very few of them have survived except in copies. To determine the exact content of the books of the Bible, therefore, we study copies—most of them copies of copies of copies.

It is only since the invention of the printing press, about the middle of the fifteenth century, that it has been easy to determine the original content of a book. The printing press first made it possible to have thousands of copies of a book all exactly alike. Before its invention no two copies of a book were ever exactly alike. Man has never attained the accuracy of the machine, and his laborious production of books in the ante-printing-press age was slow and inevitably erroneous.

If a book was first written before the fifteenth century, therefore, its original content can be determined only from a study of handwritten copies, or manuscripts. The contents of the so-called "classical literature"—the writings of ancient Greece and Rome—were determined in this fashion; and the contents of the Bible are determined in the same way. This study of ancient documents in an attempt to overcome the errors of copyists and editors and establish the exact wording of the original is a basic discipline in the study of any ancient literature. It is called "textual criticism" and is often classed with the more inoffensive areas of biblical study as "lower criticism." It is lower criticism in the sense that the foundation of a skyscraper is lower than the rest of the building which rests upon it. Its technical name, "textual criticism," is often misleading to the devout student who thinks of texts only as points of departure for the Sunday morning sermon. "Text" is used here in the sense of content. Textual criticism is interested in reconstructing the long history of the transmission of that content from its origins to our day so that the original content, or text, may be accurately restored.

It has already been suggested that the study of textual criticism faces the student of any ancient literature. Students who specialize in English literature learn its techniques to establish an accurate text of Chaucer's poems; students of Cicero, Caesar, Homer, and Vergil are forced to use either the methods or the results of textual criticism. Its devotees are the pioneers who blaze the trail for learning to travel back through the centuries to the actual words written centuries ago by gifted and inspired men. No matter what book may be the object of this study, the methods and techniques employed are the same. There may be particular tools of language or paleography needed in one case and not in another; but, in general, the methods are the same. Textual criticism of the Bible is not a thing apart. In a university seminar which attempts to establish the original wording of Chaucer's poems, F. J. A. Hort's exposition of the methods employed in textual criticism of the New Testament is required reading.

THE MATERIALS OF TEXTUAL CRITICISM

This study covers an area which is easily and naturally divided under the headings "Materials" and "Methods." The materials are ultimately manuscripts—physical, objective materials. The solidity of manuscripts and the routine nature of the elementary work in textual criticism have misled many beginners into the belief that all its methods are objective and that it is an exact science. Yet, like most other areas in the humanities, it is at some points subjective. The manuscripts are objective enough, but the methods by which they are studied and their evidence interpreted cannot be 100 per cent objective.

a) MANUSCRIPTS IN THE ORIGINAL LANGUAGE

The manuscripts studied in the textual criticism of the Bible are of three sorts: (1) manuscripts in the language of the original, (2) manuscripts of translations, and (3) manuscripts of quotations. The study of these materials is more difficult when a thousand years intervene between the date of writing the original and the date of our copies; it is less difficult when the gap is narrower. In the Greek classics the gap stretches approximately a thousand years wide; in the Latin, it is much narrower, although about three centuries separate the most favored of the Latins—Vergil—from the extant manuscripts of his works. In the case of the Hebrew manuscripts of the Old Testament, the interval is sometimes as much as seventeen hundred years; in the New Testament, it is sometimes as little as one hundred and fifty years. But the student should not rashly conclude that the New Testament text is inevitably ten times as accurate as the text of the Old Testament. The study of the text in the last fifty years has shown that the earliest period was the most fruitful in the creation of variant readings. The last thousand years can be retraced easier than the hundred that immediately followed the writing of a book. It is unlikely that any manuscript discoveries will ever carry us all the way back to the original; the most arduous part of the task of textual criticism must, therefore, be achieved with the help of translations and quotations and the use of theory—theory as sound as the careful study of all the materials can evolve.

b) TRANSLATIONS

Among the materials employed in this study, the manuscripts of translations of the Bible play an important part. This is especially the case in the Old Testament area where early translations compensate somewhat for the lack of early Hebrew manuscripts. The Pentateuch was translated into Greek in Alexandria soon after 250 B.C. The Palestinian Old Testament was translated into Syriac about A.D. 200. The Old Testament was translated into Latin before the great scholar Jerome in the latter half of the fourth century began the making of the Latin Vulgate. Such early witnesses might confidently be regarded as satisfactory substitutes for the missing Hebrew manuscripts of these periods.

But we do not possess the original manuscripts of the Greek Old Testament, or of the Syriac Old Testament, or of the Old Latin Old Testament. We have no more than fragments of the Old Latin; the oldest manuscript of any large part of the Greek Pentateuch is about five centuries later than the making of the translation; no Syriac manuscript of the Old Testament comes closer than two and a half centuries to the date given above for the making of that version. In other words, the work of establishing the original content of these versions must be carried out before the use of these versions in establishing the original content of the Hebrew Old Testament is possible.

Even if we possessed the original content of the various versions of the Bible—which for the most part we do not—the difficulty of using them in textual criticism could hardly be overestimated. Their use requires some mastery of language as well as of languages. The student must be keenly aware of what is involved in the making of a translation. He must retranslate the translation into the original language in the manner of the original translators before the evidence of the version is available.

c) QUOTATIONS

Valuable assistance in the location of varying forms of the text is given by the quotations from the Bible found in rabbinical writings, in the writings of the Church Fathers, in commentaries, etc. The valuable feature of this type of evidence is that it can usually be dated with some accuracy and located geographically with some definiteness.

Yet these values cannot be obtained without effort. We, unfortunately, do not possess the original manuscript of the writings of the rabbis and the Fathers. Critical editions (i.e., attempts to reconstruct the original content) of the Christian Fathers are steadily and systematically being prepared; valuable work is in process on rabbinical literature. But it is not yet possible to use the writings of all the early believers who quoted the Bible, with complete confidence as to the accuracy of the printed text on which you rely.

Even when you have a critical text, your task has only begun. Quotations from the Scriptures were often harmonized to contemporary standards by scribes when the rest of the text was left in its primitive form. Moreover, the value of the specific quotation for textual criticism depends to some extent upon the author's general practice in quotation. If he usually quotes in paraphrastic fashion, then the quotations from the Scripture must be studied with this in mind. If he edits as he quotes, unusual items in his quotations can be ascribed to the Scriptures only when they are supported elsewhere.

The nearer the quotations are in time to the original, the greater is their value. But, as we have already noticed, it is exactly in the earliest period that the biblical text is quoted with the greatest freedom. The first great scholar of the Christian church was Clement of Alexandria, who taught in a Christian school in that city toward the end of the second century A.D. He quotes Matthew 21:9 (*Instructor* i. 5) as follows—"Plucking branches of olives or palms, the children went forth to meet the Lord, and cried, saying, 'Hosanna to the Son of David! Blessed is he who comes in the name of the Lord.'" This is unusual in that it introduces "the children" as the ones who went out to meet Jesus. None of our biblical manuscripts (all later than Clement) mentions the children in this scene at all, although their presence inside the temple is commented on in a later section (Matt. 21:15). Should we change the manuscripts on the basis of Clement's quotation?

These "children" are found everywhere in later Christianity. We meet them in an apocryphal gospel of the fourth century. In the earliest picture of the Triumphal Entry (fifth to sixth century), they are prominent characters; and they are frequently encountered in picture, song, and story of medieval and modern Christendom. Did Clement introduce them to this role in the triumphal scene, or did he find them in the text of the early manuscript of Matthew he read? Several details indicate that Clement is responsible for the presence of the children here. In the first place, he is engaged in an argument in which it is important for him to find the Scriptures referring to Christians as "children." In the second place, he does not make a practice of exact quotation. In the third place, in the immediate context he quotes Matt. 25:33 as saying, "Let my lambs stand on my right!" although all other sources read "sheep." Yet the whole point of the passage for Clement is the use of "lambs." The change of "sheep" to "lambs" in this second passage supports the judgment that Clement changed "the crowds" to "the children" in the Triumphal Entry story. He accomplished this by transferring the children from the temple to the road outside Jerusalem. Therefore, his quotation is not of much value in any attempt to reconstruct the original form of Matt. 21:9.

UNINTENTIONAL CHANGES

In the lives of manuscripts, as of people, the first hundred years are the hardest. We have already seen that the various books which make up our Bible today were not accepted as Bible the moment they were written. The safeguards which sanctity throws around the content of a Bible were not applied to our books until they were at least a hundred years old.

To some extent in the case of the Old Testament, to a large extent in the New Testament, the cult itself lacked the organization, the trained individuals, and the interest necessary to preserve the exact wording of the documents. The New Testament is one of triplets: It was born at the same time as dogma and hierarchy. It would be more accurate to say that the doctrine of the importance of the letter of Scripture evolved with the Scripture and with the ecclesiastical organization capable of applying it to the careful preservation of the sacred text.

In Old Testament—as in New Testament—the earliest period of copying was one in which many careless errors of a scribal nature crept into the text. This is partly due to the fact that in this period the writings were not yet canonized. But in part it was due to the lack of educated and trained scribes in the service of the cult. The Hebrews were not a literary people; the early Christians came from the lower classes. The general message of a book was much more important than exactness in matters of detail.

The proof of this generalization can be seen in the wealth of variation in Old Testament text down to A.D. 200 as contrasted with its stereotyped nature since that date. It can be seen also in the earliest Greek manuscripts of the New Testament. The Beatty manuscript of Paul's letters (the oldest manuscript of Paul, written *ca.* A.D. 200), which has been published in the last few years, abounds in careless errors. Some of these are omissions; e.g., in Rom. 12:8, the words "he that shows mercy, with cheerfulness" are omitted because of the similarity between the end of this phrase and the preceding phrases. The scribe's eye passed from one ending to the other, and a line was omitted by error. Another example of this very common error can be drawn from the fourth-century Greek Bible in the Vatican library. In John 17:15, most manuscripts read:

> .... I do not ask that
> you should take them from the world, but that
> you should keep them from the evil.

But the scribe of the Vatican codex skipped from "that" to "that" and wrote:

> .... I do not ask that
> you should keep them from the evil.

In similar fashion, in both Greek and Hebrew manuscripts, letters, syllables, phrases, clauses, and sentences were omitted. Letters and words were misread. Sometimes a slip of the pen created a new reading. Very common are the errors of hearing—the confusion of two words pronounced alike. These "ear spellings" occurred not only when the manuscript was written from dictation but also when a single scribe was copying directly from the page of the exemplar. Again, if a scribe detected the omission of a word or phrase after the next word or two was written, he often inserted the omitted element at once, thus creating a variation in word order. From all of these causes, unintentional variations entered the textual tradition in large numbers.

The synagogue far surpassed the church in the

efficiency of the controls it devised and employed to preserve the content of the sacred books unchanged. From early in the Christian era down to the invention of printing, the Hebrew text varied but slightly from manuscript to manuscript. It must be understood that this is a relative judgment. Some idea of the amount of variation can be gained from the following figures. In I Chronicles, chapter 11, one manuscript has twenty-two variations from the printed text, another has seventeen, a third has eighteen, and a fourth, twenty-eight; the majority of these are scribal errors. The manuscripts of the Greek New Testament and the Latin Vulgate present many more variations in a comparable space and have a much higher proportion of significant variations.

It is possible to explain the success of the synagogue and the failure of the church by referring to the meticulous checking of the total number of words in the Hebrew books and to other similar precautions. But these are secondary phenomena. Why was the Christian church, both Greek and Latin, less interested in the accurate preservation of every letter of Scripture than the synagogue was? The answer must lie in the highly centralized authority of the Bible in Judaism; Torah monopolized religious authority. It had no such rivals in Judaism as the Christian Bible found in hierarchy and creed. Judaism had no Roman pope, no ecumenical patriarch, no Nicene Creed, no such councils as those of Carthage and Chalcedon. The very force that modernized the Jewish Bible— rabbinical interpretation—went back (at least formally) to Torah for its base of operations. Interpreters found the various minute elements of the text of great significance and, therefore, the more deserving of accurate transmission. In the Christian church, on the contrary, the clergy and the increasing body of Christian dogma shared the position of authority with the Bible; with the result that the exact wording of Scripture was never as important or as carefully preserved here as it was in Judaism.

The scribal errors mentioned above as characteristic of the earliest period were committed (in slightly less frequency) throughout the Middle Ages in the Greek and Latin manuscripts. In the Greek tradition, the last three centuries before the printing press were almost as bad as the first three, and the Latin Vulgate reached the press in an unfortunately corrupt form. Especially in these areas, the student of textual criticism is faced with the task of setting up a method or methods to overcome scribal mistakes.

STANDARD EDITIONS

The carefree attitude toward Scripture which existed in the earliest period of Christian history and in the religion of Israel in the pre-Christian period was followed by attempts to control and purify the text. This often led to the publishing of standard texts, revised texts, etc., in the manuscript period. These standard editions were prepared from the highest motives; their makers sought to remove corruptions from the text and to prevent further deterioration by establishing a standard that could be carefully preserved. The development of ecclesiastical organization, the increased efficiency of the controls used by the cult, the growth of culture—especially book culture—as the result of the impact of Hellenistic civilization on Christianity—all these supported the creation of purified and standard texts.

The number of such texts is large. In Syriac the early fifth century saw the Peshitta Version completed. The fourth century saw the making of the Latin Vulgate. As early as the second century, the Massoretic Hebrew text had been standardized. By the time of Chrysostom, the Greek text of the New Testament had been edited in at least two standard editions: one in Alexandria in Egypt, the other in Syrian Antioch.

In so far as these ecclesiastical texts checked the rate of corruption, they made a positive contribution to the history of the text. Nor can it be doubted that corruption proceeded more slowly under their repressive influence than it had in the uncontrolled period that preceded. Yet, in two ways, the making of these "revisions" makes the task of the student of the text more difficult today.

In the first place, every revision tends to displace the unrevised earlier text. Second editions replace first editions; hence the scarcity of first editions. Very often the makers or champions of the revised edition actively attacked the earlier forms of the text, destroying earlier manuscripts wherever they could find them. Thus the champions of the standard Syriac text of the Gospels destroyed manuscripts of the earlier Syriac Gospel harmony with such enthusiasm that not a single manuscript survived in the Syriac language. The champions of the Massoretic Hebrew text are at least partly responsible for the disappearance of all pre-Massoretic manuscripts of the Hebrew Bible. The difficulty caused by the lack of early manuscripts springs in part from the making of these standard versions of antiquity.

The appearance of these standard versions complicates the history of the text. In only one case, that of the Hebrew text, did the standard text dominate the ensuing tradition universally and continuously. In the Greek, Syriac, Egyptian, and Latin Bibles, the success of the revision was only partial. Not all older manuscripts were destroyed; some were corrected. And correction was never 100 per cent complete. The result is the creation of mixed texts—the curse of the manuscript student. One manuscript was corrected in some variants; another in a different set of readings. As additional manuscripts of different types were corrected to standards of varying degrees of mixture, the confusion became worse confounded. This mixture of revised with prerevised texts makes it very difficult to establish the text of the revision. The possession of the text of the revision is, however, an almost indispensable tool for the task of getting back of the revision to the primitive text.

One of the most scholarly, dramatic, and disastrous of these ancient revisions was Origen's (†A.D. 254) revision of that Greek translation of the Old Testament which is called the Septuagint. His edition is called the Hexapla and was carried out on the grand scale. Part of his purpose was to show the relation between the Hebrew text and that of the various Greek translations. He, therefore, published his work in six columns of parallel material. At the left was the Hebrew text; next, a transliteration of the Hebrew in Greek letters; then, four Greek translations: Aquila, Symmachus, the Septuagint, and Theodotion. This magnificent production had an unfortunate influence on the text of the Septuagint.

To begin with, the Hebrew column established the order of the contents; the Septuagint material was transposed to parallel the Hebrew. Moreover, Origen added to the Septuagint any material which it lacked that the Hebrew of his day contained. He usually marked this additional material by prefixing an asterisk; and, in some cases where the Greek manuscripts differed, he chose the reading that was closest to the Hebrew, without indicating the existence of the variants. Since these manuscripts had undoubtedly suffered some corruption from the influence of the Hebrew before Origen's day, the result was that he frequently preferred the worse reading. The ultimate catastrophe was that the bulk of his work prevented its mass production; hence the Septuagint column was copied out alone, in many cases without much effort to reproduce the asterisks and other diacritical marks. Thus the great difficulty in the study of the Septuagint text is to get back of Origen's Hexapla. His work, like a seven-barred gate, stands across the path that criticism must follow. The exultation with which the recent discovery of a pre-Hexaplaric manuscript was received is a by-product of the pernicious results of Origen's attempt to improve the text.

INTENTIONAL CHANGES

In the making of the standard versions, we have already seen the deliberate introduction of changes in the biblical text. While it is to be remembered that these changes were always made with the best intentions—as "corrections" or "restorations"—it must not be forgotten that the resultant text was often inferior to the unrevised text. Many an individual scribe, also, deliberately changed the text so as to correct its "errors."

Some of these changes were stylistic and grammatical. The New Testament, for example, was written in the conversational Greek of the common people. Under the pressure imposed by the growth of culture in the church (a culture that insisted on Attic Greek as the one pure dialect), scribes changed the forms of the common speech into agreement with Attic usage. Sentence structure was sometimes changed by the scribes' feeling for style. Mark 4:24 reads, "Take heed what you hear: with what measure you measure, it shall be measured to you. . . . ." In several manuscripts this is improved to, "Take heed what you hear, for with what measure you measure . . . ."

Some of these changes were intended to make the parallel accounts of the same incident agree in details. There are four accounts of Jesus' baptism. In the

Johannine account the distinctive item is the assertion that the Spirit abode upon Jesus after the baptism (1:32, 33). In many manuscripts the words "and abode upon him" are added to the accounts of the baptism in the first three gospels. In some instances the scribes carefully corrected quotations from the Old Testament in the New Testament so that the New Testament would agree with the Old Testament. The older sources of Mark 1:2 refer to "Isaiah the prophet" and proceed to quote from Malachi the prophet and then from Isaiah. Later manuscripts change "Isaiah the prophet" to "the prophets," thus making the reference to the Old Testament more accurate.

Occasionally, the Greek manuscripts of the Old Testament were edited to make them conform more explicitly to Christian faith. The ninety-fifth Psalm (ninety-six in the Septuagint) was identified as a messianic Psalm, probably because of the reference to the Lord (God) coming in judgment. The tenth verse of this Psalm reads, "Say among the nations, the Lord reigns." Some enthusiastic Christian scribes have made this a reference to the crucifixion by adding the words "from the tree" (i.e., the cross) after the verb "reigns."

Not only was book harmonized with book, but the Scriptures were harmonized also with liturgical practice. In the Greek church, on the fourth evening of Lent, Matt. 7:7 was read after Mark 11:26. The same combination of passages was read quite frequently on saints' days, especially on December 9.

As a result of this, some manuscripts of the Gospels follow Mark 11:26 with Matt. 7:7. The same natural influence of liturgy upon the text can be seen in the addition of the doxology to the Lord's Prayer.

Some intentional changes were purely explanatory in character, intended to clear up obscurities in the text. They were written on the margin of the manuscript or between the lines; from these positions some of them crept into the text itself. They usually are brief additions.

A larger number of changes were of a dogmatic nature. Where the scribe found the sacred text saying something unworthy of deity, he knew it was wrong and proceeded to correct it as well as he could. The development of paraphrases for the divine name in the Old Testament, the avoidance of anthropomorphisms in the versions of the Old Testament, etc., are all examples of this. The Old Testament scribes had the term *Tiqqune sopherim* for their deliberate changes made in the interest of dogma or decency. An interesting example is Hab. 1:12, where "you do not die," said to God was changed to "we shall not die." The original form of the verse was, "Are you not from everlasting, O Yahweh, my God? My Holy One, you do not die." Another example is the change in Gen. 18:22 from "The Lord was yet standing before Abraham" to "Abraham was yet standing before the Lord." Similar deliberate changes were made by the scribes who copied the New Testament. Mark 13:32 reads, "But of that day and that hour knoweth no man, no, not the angels which are in

heaven, neither the Son, but the Father." Several
New Testament manuscripts omit the words "neither
the Son" because of the implication of limitation of
Jesus' knowledge.

Not only theological doctrines but also social
feeling affected the text. This was especially true in
the earliest period when the transmission was least
controlled. Early Christianity became anti-Semitic
before it was one hundred years old, and the word
"anti-Semitic" is used here to mean dominated by
prejudice and passion in general attitudes toward the
Jews. In a manuscript of the Old Syriac version,
called the Curetonian manuscript, a striking change
is made in Matt. 1:21 because of this anti-Semitic
bias. Most manuscripts read, "You shall call his
name Jesus, for he shall save his people . . . ." but
this manuscript changes "his people" to "the world,"
thereby removing one Jewish element from the
gospel. I have called attention elsewhere to the
thoroughness with which the author of the Fourth
Gospel has read Jesus out of Judaism.

The early Christian believers were sensitive to the
charge that Jesus was a criminal because he had been
executed by Roman authority in the most shameful
manner possible. They did everything they could to
reduce the reproach of the cross. Luke 23:32 says,
"There were also two others, malefactors, led with
him to be executed." Nothing but the final *s* on
"others" and the commas save the reader of the
English version from assuming that this implies that
Jesus was a malefactor. The possibility of reading the

passage this way in the ancient languages was even
stronger. The vast mass of our earliest New Testament manuscript text was written without commas,
thus the risk of reading that Jesus was a malefactor
was much greater. Some Old Latin manuscripts and
the Sinaitic Syriac manuscript omit the word "other"
or "others," thus removing all implication that Jesus
was a criminal. The Fourth Gospel achieves the
same result by retaining "others" and omitting
"malefactors."

METHODS

How is the student of the text to get back to the
original content of the Bible in spite of the intentional
and unintentional changes made during the centuries
of its transmission? Many methods have been suggested, but none is self-sufficient. Only when the
shortcomings of the various techniques are realized,
can their virtues be combined with reasonable success.

There are several 100 per cent objective methods,
and they are all worthless. One is to count the number of manuscripts supporting one reading and the
number supporting the rival reading and then to
accept the reading supported by the larger number of
manuscripts. There is one drawback to the adoption
of this method. As with people so with manuscripts—
those with the worst character often have the most
children. One thousand descendants of a very care-
lessly written manuscript do not outweigh ten descendants of a carefully written manuscript. In the
last fifty years this method has been repudiated by

the world of scholarship. The statement that "most manuscripts" read "so-and-so" is not decisive.

Equally objective but even less defensible is the choice of the oldest manuscript as representing the original text. It would be possible to publish a Bible whose content was determined solely on the basis of date; that is, the reading with the most ancient attestation would be chosen. This is never seriously considered by scholarship but is occasionally attempted by those who have gulped down one hasty mouthful of manuscript lore. Its repudiation by the authorities in this field rises from their recognition of two facts: (1) the period of wildest variation was the earliest period and (2) no one manuscript (not even the oldest) is entirely correct. The antiquity of a reading is not in itself a decisive criterion of authenticity.

A much more popular and significant method is called the genealogical method from its attempt to trace the ancestry of manuscripts. If manuscripts were all related to one another in the pattern son-father-grandfather-greatgrandfather, etc., it would be a simple matter to establish a family tree for each late manuscript and then group the families into clans and tribes and nations, to identify the "father" of each nation, and finally to find the parent of these fathers in the original manuscript. Theoretically, this is accomplished by the genealogical method as applied to manuscripts. But, actually, the method has not been applied to biblical manuscripts as manuscripts.

The reasons for this are manifold. In the Old Testament there are so few manuscripts of any antiquity that the family tree could be held together only by the most extensive use of all the devices of tree surgery. In the New Testament there are so many manuscripts that the tree would have to be taller than the sequoias with a tangle of branches suggesting a cross between the banyan and the crab apple. A beginning has been made by the identification of a few families (with six to twenty members) and their tentative grouping in larger units; but the real work on a genealogical scheme of New Testament manuscripts is still to be done.

More serious obstacles to the employment of the genealogical method exist in the complex nature of relationships between manuscripts. The mixture of texts that results from "correction" has already been mentioned. When part of the readings throughout one manuscript come from one ancestor and part from a very different ancestor, and when this is the case with scores and hundreds of manuscripts, the complexity of a chart that would represent ancestry is bewildering and intimidating. Another type of mixture springs from the use of two or more manuscripts in sequence in the making of a manuscript. Matthew may have been copied from one source, Mark from another, Luke from a third, and John from a fourth— thus one manuscript of the Four Gospels would have four fathers.

Nor would four fathers be an extravagant number, especially in the early period—and (in the New

Testament area) the latest period. The early and famous Washington manuscript of the Gospels not only has different ancestors in different Gospels but also switches parents within the Gospel of Mark. The Four Gospels of Karahissar from the late thirteenth century is descended from eight different "fathers," and in at least two sections the text was corrected by still other types.

It is no wonder, therefore, that the genealogical method is more often applied to variants than to manuscripts. This use will be discussed below, but it should be noted here that this method has also rendered valuable service in the study of the broad general areas of manuscript study. Here it has served to take certain main groups of manuscripts back to the later edge of the primitive period. This has been done only in a broad, loose, general fashion; and the genealogical method alone will never carry us over the deep chasm of the primitive period.

Another valuable method is the internal criticism of readings. Down through the generations of careful study of manuscripts, scholars have set forth longer and shorter lists of "canons" or rules to guide the student in that choice between alternative readings which is the central task of textual criticism. Some of these sound paradoxical, and most of them have little practical value. Two of the most famous are "the more difficult reading is to be preferred" and "the shorter reading is the older." The first springs from the assumption that a scribe would never intentionally make a reading more difficult. But what of unintentional change? And would readings that seem difficult to us always seem difficult to all the scribes who have worked on the text? If this rule were followed rigorously in all cases, the original text would approach unintelligibility. The second rule ignores the common tendency of scribes to omit either intentionally (in times of revision or in the primitive period) or unintentionally. Suppose the student must choose between two readings—one long and one short, and the long one is the more difficult. He must either find additional rules or fall back on his own judgment of the relative value of these rules.

Additional rules can be found in the combination of genealogical method with study of variants. All the variations in one passage are assembled; the student then chooses that one which best explains all the others. In other words, he constructs a family tree of variants. In Mark 1:12–13 some manuscripts read, "And immediately the Spirit drove him out into the desert. And he was in the desert forty days. ...." Others read, ".... into the desert. And he was there forty days. ....." Still others read, ".... into the desert. And he was there in the desert forty days. ....." Obviously, the third is the child of the first and the second. The choice between the other two, so far as this rule is concerned, then depends on a judgment as to whether "into the desert. And he was in the desert ...." would be changed to "into the desert. And he was there ...." or vice versa.

To assist in such difficult decisions the further rule is employed that that variant is to be chosen which best fits the context—which is most at home in the author's style, vocabulary, ideas, and purpose. These two rules are the most practical and valuable for internal study of readings.

The last method is called "conjectural emendation." When the text as preserved in all the manuscripts does not make sense, it is clear that (1) we are too stupid to understand it, or (2) the author wrote nonsense, or (3) the original reading has been lost. Since we usually think too highly of ourselves and the author to accept (1) or (2), we try to restore the lost reading by conjecture. This is employed more rarely in the New Testament area than in the Old Testament for obvious reasons. The greater number and greater antiquity of New Testament manuscripts makes it less probable that many readings have been lost; this judgment is objectively supported by the large number of unintelligible passages in the Hebrew Old Testament and the small number of such passages in the Greek New Testament.

All students of the biblical text have admitted the legitimacy of conjectural emendation. Even the sacred name of Hort can be quoted in support of its application to the New Testament in moderation. In *The New Testament: An American Translation*, Professor Goodspeed has translated several conjectural emendations. One of the most striking is in I Pet. 3:19, where he accepts the suggestion of Rendel Harris that the name of Enoch has dropped from all manuscripts. The omission would be caused by the similarity of the two lines ENOK(AI) and ENOCH, which are easily confused in Greek uncial characters.

The sixteenth edition of Nestle's Greek text of the New Testament records about two hundred conjectural emendations. These are given in the critical apparatus below the text; in ninety instances they are accompanied by the name of the scholar who first suggested them; in a few cases they are marked by Nestle with the symbol used to designate readings "which, according to widespread opinion, might be original." An example is Matt. 2:6, "And you Bethlehem, land of Judah, ..." which by the addition of one letter in the Greek text reads (more sensibly), "And you Bethlehem of the land of Judah. . . . ."

A striking conjectural emendation in the Old Testament is that of Professor Arnold in I Sam. 14:18. The Hebrew reads, "And Saul said to Ahijah, Bring hither the ark of God, for the ark of God was in that day and the children of Israel." The Greek version reads, ". . . . hither the Ephod; for he bore the Ephod in that day before Israel." The conjecture is that the Hebrew was deliberately corrupted to hide the fact that there were many arks in ancient Israel, the Greek version obtaining the same result by translating "ark" as "Ephod." If "ark" be substituted for "Ephod" in the Greek, the original sense of the passage is recovered.

Another emendation of a famous Old Testament passage is made in Isa. 9:3, which has been read in three ways. The Massoretic Hebrew text reads (as the King James Version translates), "Thou hast multiplied the nation, and not increased the joy; they joy before thee according to the joy in harvest, as men rejoice when they divide the spoil." All the rest of the verse argues against the authenticity of the negative before "increased the joy." As a recognition of this, the Revisers read it as, "Thou hast multiplied the nation; thou hast increased their joy, etc." This change is made possible by reading *lo'* as *lô*. But this reading has been further improved by attaching this *lo'* to the preceding word, which gives the meaning: "Thou hast multiplied rejoicing; thou hast increased joy, etc." A slight change in word division restores the clear meaning of the original.

By conjectural emendation, by genealogical study of manuscripts and variants, by a careful study of each manuscript's distinctive characteristics, by the help of versions and quotations, and by the most searching scrutiny of all the variant readings, the text of the Bible is established. No one method is employed to the exclusion of the others; internal and external criticism support one another's hands. In the objective part of the task the law is accuracy; in the subjective, common sense.

ACHIEVEMENTS

By the use of these methods, the corrupt form of the Greek text of the New Testament which ruled from A.D. 1516 to 1880 has been repudiated. In A.D. 1516 Erasmus rushed through the press an edition of the Greek New Testament based on a mere handful of late manuscripts, none earlier than the tenth century. Except for minor modifications, this text remained the standard Greek text of the New Testament through the middle of the nineteenth century.

It is this type of text which was translated to make the King James Version. But throughout this period the manuscript resources were being constantly enriched by discovery and study, and methods were being improved and refined. Tischendorf's discovery of a fourth-century Greek Bible on Mount Sinai dramatized the value of the new resources in effective fashion, and the second half of the nineteenth century saw the production of new editions of the Greek Testament based on hundreds of manuscripts, scores of them earlier than the earliest used by Erasmus.

The Massoretic Hebrew text of the Old Testament was at the same time being revised into greater accuracy, and the versions of the Old Testament have been used to make significant improvements in the English Bible. Better methods and new materials have each done their part to carry the content of our Bible back closer and closer to its original form. Where the King James Version represented the text of the Bible as it existed from the tenth to the fifteenth century, the revised versions and to a still higher degree some of the modern-speech translations go back to the Bible as it existed in the late third or early fourth century. Finality has not been attained, nor will it be attained in our lifetime. But the great wealth of second- and third-century manuscripts discovered in the last decade and the slow but constant increase in our knowledge of the significance of all the sources will make a still better text possible for our children.

BIBLIOGRAPHY ON TRANSMISSION

GENERAL

PRICE, I. M. *The Ancestry of Our English Bible: An Account of Manuscripts, Texts, and Versions of the Bible* (2d rev. ed. by W. A. IRWIN and A. P. WIKGREN). New York: Harper & Bros., 1949.

A fine elementary treatment of the transmission of the Bible. Good bibliographies.

KENYON, SIR FREDERIC. *Our Bible and the Ancient Manuscripts* (rev. by W. A. ADAMS). New York: Harper & Bros., 1958.

A fine introduction to this area of study. Good selection of plates.

JEFFERY, A., "Text and Ancient Versions of the Old Testament," and COLWELL, ERNEST C., "Text and Ancient Versions of the New Testament," in *The Interpreter's Bible*, Vol. I. Nashville: Abingdon, 1952.

CLARK, KENNETH L., "The Transmission of the New Testament," and TREVER, JOHN C. "Illustrated History of the Biblical Text," in *The Interpreter's Bible*, Vol. XII. Nashville: Abingdon, 1952.

ADVANCED

a) MANUALS

METZGER, B. M. *The Text of the New Testament: Its Transmission, Corruption, and Restoration.* New York: Oxford University Press, 1964.

A comprehensive discussion by an outstanding leader of current study.

ROBERTS, B. J. *The Old Testament Text and Versions: The Hebrew Text in Transmission and the History of the Ancient Versions.* Cardiff: University of Wales Press, 1951.

Comprehensive, scholarly. Contains data on important manuscripts. Good bibliography.

WÜRTHWEIN, ERNST. *The Text of the Old Testament.* Oxford: Blackwell, 1957.

Especially helpful in explaining the *sigla* and apparatus of Kittel's *Biblia Hebraica*. Contains data on important manuscripts. 40 plates.

VAGANAY, L.—DUPLACY, JEAN. *Le texte du Nouveau Testament.*
Forthcoming. (The translation to be published by Doubleday
replaces the translation of Vaganay by B. V. MILLER.)

Duplacy is a leading scholar in this field, and his work deserves the
most serious attention.

KENYON, SIR FREDERIC. *Handbook to the Textual Criticism of the
New Testament* (2d ed., 1912). Grand Rapids: Eerdman, n.d.

Good introductory survey of materials and methods as they were
known in 1912.

LAKE, K. *The Text of the New Testament* (6th rev. ed. by SILVA
NEW). London: Christopher, 1928.

Brief, concise introduction by a master of the subject.

b) CRITICAL EDITIONS

I. NEW TESTAMENT

WESTCOTT, B. F., and HORT, F. J. A. *The New Testament in the
Original Greek*, Vol. I: *The Text;* Vol. II: *Introduction and Appendix.* New York: Harper & Bros., 1882.

This text has practically become the standard text of the Greek New
Testament in England and, to a lesser degree, in America. The text itself
has no critical apparatus, but the second volume gives a classic discussion
of methods and principles of textual criticism. The lexicon by Hickie,
which is often bound in with the text in Macmillan's edition, is the worst
lexicon of the Greek New Testament in use today. Students who buy the
text volume should buy the edition without the lexicon.

EBERHARD NESTLE'S *Novum Testamentum Graece cum apparatu
critico curavit* (25th ed. by ERWIN NESTLE and K. ALAND).
Stuttgart: Privilegierte Württembergische Bibelanstalt, 1963.

This is the best edition for classroom use. It is less expensive than any
of its rivals. It gives variant readings in a critical apparatus which is constantly revised. Cross-references are given in the margins, Old Testament
sources being identified. Verse divisions are plainly indicated. Most of the
equipment of the medieval Greek manuscripts is reproduced. The text is
derived from those of Weiss, Tischendorf, and Hort; it is quite close to
that of Westcott and Hort.

TISCHENDORF, C. *Novum Testamentum Graece . . . . editio critica
octava maior.* Leipzig: Heinrich's, 1869–72.

A critical text with a good apparatus, now antiquated by the discoveries of the last half-century. The text is in general similar to that of Westcott and Hort.

VON SODEN, H. *Die Schriften des Neuen Testaments in ihrer ältesten erreichbaren Textgestalt,* Vol. I. Berlin: Glaue, 1902–10. Vol. II. Göttingen: Vandenhoeck & Ruprecht, 1913.

Von Soden's theory of the history of the text has been severely criticized and generally repudiated by scholars. As a result, his text has not been accepted for scholarly study. But his work is an invaluable introduction to the study of the medieval manuscripts of the New Testament.

WORDSWORTH, I., and WHITE, H. I. *Novum Testamentum domini nostri Jesu Christi Latine.* Oxford: Clarendon Press, 1889–1954.

This is now the outstanding critical edition of the Vulgate. A manual edition without lengthy introductions and apparatus was published in 1911 (corrected edition 1920) at the Clarendon Press, Oxford.

2. OLD TESTAMENT

KITTEL, R. *Biblia Hebraica* (7th ed. rev. by P. KAHLE, A. ALT, and O. EISSFELDT). Stuttgart: Privilegierte Württembergische Bibelanstalt, 1951.

A sound critical edition of the Hebrew Scriptures, with brief apparatus. It includes readings of Qumran Isaiah and Habakkuk.

RAHLFS, A. *Septuaginta.* Stuttgart: Privilegierte Württembergische Bibelanstalt, 1935.

This appears in two forms—a two-volume student edition and a one-volume de luxe edition. The text is based on the three oldest manuscripts as a primary source, but much additional evidence is given in the apparatus. This edition is cheaper, more legible, and more up to date than that of Swete.

BROOKE, A. E., and McLEAN, N. *The Old Testament in Greek According to the Text of Codex Vaticanus.* Cambridge: At the University Press, 1906——.

This larger Cambridge edition repeats and improves in details the text made familiar to students for the last generation in the manual edition of H. B. Swete. In this larger work, the text is supplemented by the evidence of a valuable selected apparatus, which includes all the uncials, all early versions, much important patristic evidence, and a small group of minuscules. The last fasciculus to appear contained Esther, Judith, Tobit.

RAHLFS, A. *Septuaginta*. (This series began with Genesis, then skipped to Psalms and continues through the second half of the LXX to XVI. 2 Susanna, Daniel, Bel et Draco. Thus it postpones duplication of the Cambridge LXX.) Göttingen: Vandenhoeck & Ruprecht, 1926——.

For bibliography on the Dead Sea Scrolls, the Bodmer Papyri and the Gnostic documents from Nag Hammadi, see chapter vii.

Chapter III
The Translation of the Bible

WHEN the modern American Christian reads the sermons of John Wesley, he is reading the sermons of John Wesley; when he reads the religious essays of G. K. Chesterton, he is reading what Chesterton wrote. But when he reads the Bible, he is not reading the Bible but a translation of the Bible into English. He knows the Scriptures only at second hand; he does not know the Bible itself. Some scholar has come between him and the original; for the meaning of that original, he is at the mercy of a translator or a group of translators. He is held at this distance from the original by his ignorance of Hebrew, Aramaic, and Greek—the languages in which the books of his Bible were written.

REASONS FOR TRANSLATING

a) MISSIONARY

The rapid expansion of the Christian religion created situations in which the need of translations of the Scriptures was felt strongly. The twentieth-century Christian can sympathize with his predecessors in their recognition of this need. The Christian religion has come a long distance in time and territory from the cities of Corinth, Philippi, and Rome—cities in which Christian churches read the letters that Paul wrote to them in Greek. It has come still farther away from the background and language of the books of the Old Testament. This expansion of the cult to groups that did not know the language of its sacred writings demanded the production of translations.

The work of supplying this need of the expanding cult began long before Christianity came to Birmingham and Chicago. Before the Christian church was two hundred years old, its missionaries had gone beyond the limits of the Greek-speaking centers of the Mediterranean world. This was partly due to a decrease in the use of Greek and an increase in the use of the old national languages during the period of the church's expansion. Christian penetration into the back-country sections of Africa and Syria called forth translations of the gospels into Latin and Syriac. Ever since then translation has been a recognized missionary activity in the Christian church. The great Bible societies of the present day publish the Scriptures in literally hundreds of languages.

b) LINGUISTIC CHANGE

Another element that called forth translations of the Bible was change in linguistic usage. The only certain thing that can be said about the future of any language that is being spoken is that it will change. It is equally certain that they have all changed and that all living languages are in constant process of change. The changes occur in form, in the mechanics of sentence structure, in the meaning of words, etc.

The changes in the meanings of words are often so great that they make the tracing of etymologies a fascinating sport. "Sincere" comes from two Latin words meaning "without wax"; "treacle" ("molasses" in the United States) goes back to a Greek adjective meaning "pertaining to a wild beast." There is little rhyme or reason to some of these changes, but the student may be able to understand why all words that mean "at once" today will mean "after a little while" tomorrow.

In Shakespeare's day the word "presently" meant "at once," as the following example from Hamlet shows. As Polonius urges the king and queen out of the way with the words, "I'll board him presently," Hamlet enters and is *at once* addressed by Polonius (II,2). But when the modern husband who is asked by his wife to fix the curtain in the dining-room mutters, "I'll fix it presently," she knows and he knows that he has not promised to fix it "at once."

Words that refer to odors inevitably come to mean bad odors, no matter how neutral their origin. Dryden could speak of "clouds of savory stench" without being humorous, but the modern poet cannot. That Spenser whose *Faerie Queene* is so delightful to some scholars and so boring to the college undergraduate wrote of his bride in the *Epithalamion* (l. 148), "Loe, where she comes along with portly pace!" Yet she was not a large woman, nor did he mean to imply that she was stout. The word "portly" in his day meant—among other things—dignified, stately; today it always implies stoutness of girth.

Similar changes in the meaning of English words

make much of the King James Version of the Bible obscure today. The obscurity in the following passages is due to linguistic change in the English language, not to any obscurity in the original: "My eyes prevent the night watches" (Ps. 119:148); ".... a valley with running water, which is neither eared nor sown . . . ." (Deut. 21:4). "Prevent" no longer means "anticipate," nor does "eared" today mean "plowed." When the makers of the King James Version asked, "Who can find a virtuous woman?" (Prov. 31:10), they were no more cynical about women than the Revisers, who said "A worthy woman who can find?" or the maker of the American Translation, who said, "If one can find a good wife, she is worth far more than corals." The word "virtuous" when applied to a woman had a much broader meaning in the days of King James than it has today.

These examples give an indication of the way in which change in language makes the sacred text obscure. Over longer periods of time, or in periods of sudden linguistic change, the need for a new translation is even more manifest. Thus Hebrew became a dead language for the Jews in the period following the Exile, although its prestige as the language of the Scriptures gave it a limited existence, especially in Palestine. But the majority of the people needed a translation, which was supplied in Palestine in oral translation into Aramaic, the contemporary language; and in the Dispersion by a translation into Greek. This translation was begun in Alexandria three centuries before the Christian Era. The Jews of that city were familiar with Greek as the spoken language of the metropolis; many of them were bilingual; some probably knew Greek alone. But the Hebrew Bible was unintelligible to the vast majority of them; they needed a new translation. The translations into Anglo-Saxon are of no use to the English-speaking Christian today for the same reason; they are written in a dead language. The changes in the English language—especially the changes that occurred from 1525 to 1900—have been influential in creating new translations: the revised versions and the modern-speech translations of this century.

A student of translations has observed that the language of a translation ages more rapidly than does the language of works that are native to the tongue. What in an original composition is an ornament (the quaintness of language now become archaic, etc.) is a defect in a translation whose primary function is to convey meaning. Hence no translation of any classic is ever final, and periodic translation is the intelligent ideal.

c) COMPETITION AND STRESS

New translations of the Bible spring not only from the missionary needs of the church and the aging of language but also from the confusion and stress caused by the presence of rival translations, or by the presence of translations that clash with contemporary faith. One of the important elements in the situation that produced the Latin translation of Jerome was the presence of a large number of varying earlier Latin translations. Sophronius Eusebius Hieronymus

(Jerome to us) may have exaggerated slightly when he insisted that there were as many different Latin translations of the Bible as there were Latin manuscripts of the Bible, for it must be remembered that he was the champion of yet another translation. Yet the support given the undertaking by the pope shows that official Christianity regarded these contradictory versions as a liability; the hierarchy was anxious to reduce variety in translation to uniformity.

In the earliest decades of Christian history, Christians and Jews alike used the Septuagint translation of the Old Testament into Greek as the authoritative Bible. It was, in fact, from the Jews that the Christians received this version. The welcome they gave it was too warm to please the Jews; for the rivalry between the two cults was bitter, and the use of allegorical interpretation made it possible for the Christian Fathers to baptize the Septuagint itself. Its language was appealed to in support of Christian doctrine until the pious Jew in desperation demanded another, more accurate version. In Isa. 7:14 the Septuagint prediction that a "virgin" would bear a son was hailed by the Christian as proof that Jesus was the Messiah; while the Jew cried for a translation that would more accurately represent the Hebrew word "maiden." The second century saw several such translations prepared to meet this need; the most famous of these is the one attributed to a certain Aquila.

In the middle of the nineteenth century in the United States there was a strong and sometimes bitter debate between various Protestant denominations as to the mode of baptism which was scriptural. Some denominations permitted baptism by immersion, by sprinkling, or by pouring; others permitted baptism by immersion alone, claiming that this was the sole scriptural method. The intensity of feeling aroused can be seen in the following title: *Immersionists against the Bible, or the Babel Builders Confounded, in an Exposition of the Origin, Design, Tactics and Progress of the New Version Movement of Campbellites and Other Baptists*. This work was published by N. H. Lee at Nashville, Tennessee, in 1856.

Through the verbiage of this polemical title one can clearly see that the authority of the Scriptures was important to this dispute, and that it was inevitable that sooner or later a version of the New Testament would appear which would translate the Greek word "baptize" by "immerse." A revision of the King James Version which changed the translation at this point as well as elsewhere was undertaken by the American Bible Union in 1860; the Gospels appeared in 1862, the entire New Testament in 1865. In these editions (as also in the second edition, 1866), not only is the verb *baptizo* translated "immerse" but John the Baptizer appears as "John the Immerser" in Matt. 3:1, etc. In later editions the verb alone is translated with "immerse." This is the case in the "edition with immerse," a revision of the Bible Union Version, published by the American Baptist Publication Society at Philadelphia in 1885.

It may be that the intensity of the debate weakened

in the rank and file of the believers with the passing of time, for at the same time and place the Baptist Society published an edition with "baptize" as the translation of the Greek *baptizo*. The two editions were otherwise identical; they are distinguished by a label on the title-page; one is marked "Edition with Immerse," the other "[Baptize]."

In Elizabethan England the Protestants—especially the more zealous reformers—were able to read the Bible at home in one of several translations made into the English from Greek, Hebrew, and other sources. Preachers read these vernacular versions in the pulpit and quoted them copiously in their sermons. In the stress of that era of change, many of these sermons were attacks on Rome. It is not, therefore, strange that champions of the Roman faith found this use of the English versions trying. The popularity of these new translations—especially the Geneva Bible—among the masses of the people probably led some of the Roman Catholics to an unauthorized reading for themselves. Further stress was introduced into the situation by the recent decree of the Council of Trent (1546), which had established the Latin version of Jerome (the Vulgate) as the authoritative form of the Roman Catholic Bible. But none of the English translations in use then was translated from the Vulgate. Under the pressure of these "heretical" versions (as the translators say in their Preface), a translation of the New Testament from the Latin Vulgate was made at Reims, and—later—the Old Testament was translated at Douai. Thus missionary activity and natural change in language have been joined by cult needs in times of competition as causes of new translations of the Bible.

THE TASK OF THE TRANSLATOR

The production of a new translation always leads the translator into difficulties and problems. His first task—and not his easiest one—is to define the work he is about to do. Is he going to make a new translation from the best editions of the Bible in the original languages? Or is he to be content with a revision, a polishing, of an earlier translation? The latter ideal has controlled most English translations of the Scriptures, and in most of them the rule has been not to make as many improvements as possible but rather to make only those improvements which could not be avoided. But, even if the natural conservatism of all religions is overcome and a new translation is decided on, the most difficult problems still await solution.

a) DEFINITION OF THE TASK

The most baffling problem of all is: What is translation? How does it differ from paraphrase? Is it, in any sense, interpretation? What is an accurate translation? Is a translation literal when it translates word by word, or phrase by phrase, or sentence by sentence? Must poetry be translated into poetry? Is it possible to translate the "spirit" or "feeling" of a work without translating its words? How many words in one language are the exact equivalent of similar words in another? What should the translator do with proper nouns that have lost significance? What should be done with ancient weights and measures? Can a translation be twice as long as the original and still be a translation?

It is generally agreed that a translation must be faithful to the original; agreement vanishes when this fidelity is defined. The sanest ideal is summed up in the adage: "As literal as possible, as free as is necessary." Some freedom is a necessity for idiomatic and intelligible translation; the translation of units smaller than sentences or independent clauses seldom permits the attainment of clarity or idiomatic treatment. But the freedom of the translator is intolerable when it produces "libertine" translations.

The twenty-fourth book of the *Iliad* ends with the line, "Such was the burial of Hector, master of horses." Alexander Pope, master of the heroic couplet in English, translated this as follows:

> Such honors Ilion to her hero paid
> And peaceful slept the mighty Hector's shade.

Who said anything about Ilion? What has become of the horses? And how does Pope know that Hector's shade slept peacefully? This is something more than translation. The doubling of the quantity in the process of translation is here seen for the dangerous thing it is. Fidelity in translation includes fidelity to the amount of the original. The introduction of proper names not in the text is still another misleading feature of too-free translation. Fortunately, there is almost no translation of this kind in the English versions of the Bible. The innate conservatism of the religious has kept the translator closer to the text.

The outstanding fault of translations of the Bible is that they are too close to the original—too literal. The ideal of absolute fidelity may lead the translator as far astray as too much love of freedom. In Hebrew the pronoun "I" has a longer and a shorter form, and the verb is frequently omitted in such simple affirmations as "I (am) the king." The Septuagint translator of some of the Former Prophets was led by these facts and his desire for fidelity to translate these two forms of the pronoun consistently in two ways. Where the longer form occurred, he translated it as "I am"; while he regularly translated the shorter form with "I." This causes no difficulty in sentences like "I am thy God" but is disastrous in "I am said unto him. . . . ." Every student of this version has been exasperated at some time or other by the translator's refusal to perform his function: in the substitution of transliteration for translation. Transliteration may be faithful, but it does not glow with meaning.

The English versions of the Bible have produced literalisms as unintelligible as any in the Septuagint. The obscurity that results from an unintelligent fidelity to each word of the original can be seen in the American Revised Version of Eph. 1:3-14, where participial phrases alternate with relative clauses through a sentence of two hundred and sixty-eight words that conveys the minimum of meaning. But the champion of champions in literalness is the Douai version (also called the Reims). The translators' conception of their task is expressed in the following lines from their Preface:

We presume not to mollify the speeches or phrases, but religiously keep them word for word, and point for point, for fear of missing or restraining the sense of the Holy Ghost to our fancy.

Such a principle applied to the Latin Vulgate produced incredible English.

This translation is much clearer in the Gospels than it is in the rest of the New Testament; this is due, at least in part, to the greater simplicity of the original in the gospel section. The following passages from the Epistles give some idea of the degree of unintelligibility that can be attained by literal translation. Rom. 1:28 f., "God delivered them up into a reprobate sense: to do those things that are not convenient: replenished with all iniquity, malice, fornication, avarice, wickedness, ... detractours, odible to God, contumelious." Rom. 2:11, ". . . . for there is no acception of persons with God." Rom. 2:14–16, "For when the Gentiles which have not the Law, naturally do those things which are of the Law: the same not having the Law, themselves are a law to themselves: who shew the work of the Law written in their hearts, their conscience giving testimony to them and among themselves mutually their thoughts accusing, or also defending, in the day when God shall judge the secrets of men. . . . ." Rom. 5:14, ". . . . that sinned not after the similitude of the prevarication of Adam. . . . ." Titus 3:1, "Be subject to Princes and Potestates to obey at a word. . . . ." Philem. 6, ". . . . that the communication of thy faith may be made evident in the agnition of all good that is in you in Christ Jesus. For I have had great joy and consolation in thy charitie, because the bowels of the sainctes have rested by thee, brother. For the which thing having great confidence in Christ Jesus to command thee that which pertaineth to the purpose: for charitie rather I beseech, whereas thou art such an one as Paul being old and now prisoner also of Jesus Christ." This cannot be read without a Latin lexicon. Even with the help of such a lexicon, one cannot easily grasp its meaning. The excessive fidelity of the translators has betrayed the reader.

This extreme literalness as an ideal sometimes holds the translators to a text which makes no sense whatever, when the use of conjectural emendation—or a little more freedom in translation—would solve the difficulties. Note the increase in intelligibility in the following verse (Ps. 45:5) as it moves from translation to translation. The Bishops' Bible: "Thyne arrowes are sharp: a people the king's enemies shall submit in heart themselves unto thee." The King James Bible: "Thine arrowes are sharp in the heart of the king's enemies; whereby the people fall under thee." The Douai Bible: "Thy sharp arrowes, the peoples underneath thee shall fal into the hartes of the king's enemies." The American Revised: "Thine arrows are sharp; the peoples fall under thee; they are in the heart of the king's enemies." The American Translation: "May your sharp arrows be in the midst of the king's foes! May peoples fall under you!"

A passage famous for its obscurity is Eccles. 12:11.

The King James Version loses none of the obscurity in its rendering: "The words of the wise are as goads, and as nails fastened by the masters of assemblies, which are given from one shepherd."

The dangers implicit in obscure or ambiguous translation are very real; naturally, they are greater for the pastor or layman who must rely on his English version alone for his understanding of the Scriptures. There is no more dangerous passage in the so-called "standard versions" (King James, English Revised, and American Revised) than Matt. 26:27. These versions agree in rendering this verse, "And he [Jesus] took a cup, and gave thanks, and gave to them saying, Drink ye all of it. . . . ." A recent inspirational article in a denominational weekly expounds the words "Drink ye all of it' " through six columns. The author takes these words as a command to the disciples to drink all of the wine in the cup. "If they drank only part of the wine they were only partially consecrated, while if they drank all of the wine they were completely consecrated. So Jesus said, 'Drink ye all of it!' " But the "ye all" of these versions is the ancestor of our modern southern idiom "you all." It means "all of you"; there is no ambiguity whatever in the Greek, which says plainly, "all of you drink of it."

b) SELECTION OF A TEXT

The translator cannot escape the problems of textual criticism outlined in the preceding chapter. He must select a text to translate. The best translation in the world—best in fidelity and in idiomatic result—will not be satisfactory if it translates a text repudiated as inaccurate by the world of scholarship. Water from a tainted reservoir may be delivered through the most modern of distribution systems and yet not meet the approval of the board of health. The inaccuracy of the Greek and Hebrew texts behind the King James Version makes it impossible for the modern student to use that version in any serious study of the Bible. The fundamental cause of the making of the Revised Version was the increase in the knowledge of the manuscript tradition of both Testaments, but especially of the New Testament. The discovery, publication, and study of one ancient manuscript was followed by that of another throughout the first half of the nineteenth century. Tischendorf's discovery of the famous Codex Sinaiticus brought the attention of the pious public to the progress that was being made in improving the accuracy of the Greek New Testament. No Greek manuscript behind the King James Version was older than the eleventh century; the Greek text upon which the Revisers worked rested on more manuscripts earlier than the eleventh century than the total number employed in the making of the King James Version. Admirers of Elizabethan prose will still cherish the King James Version for its English style; the unintelligent will still regard it as *the* Bible by which all other versions are to be evaluated; but the student who wants to know what the Bible actually says will turn to more modern and accurate translations.

Most of the translations made in the last fifty years rest on texts of comparable quality. In the New Testament the Greek texts translated are all fairly close to the edition of Westcott and Hort. This is true of the English Revised Version, the American Revised Version, the Twentieth Century New Testament, Weymouth's New Testament in Modern Speech, Goodspeed's American Translation, and others. There are some striking exceptions. A West Coast group in 1919–24 produced a translation made from the three oldest manuscripts (Vaticanus, Sinaiticus, and Alexandrinus), translating their agreements as the "Concordant Version." We have discussed the futility of such a method of selecting a text in the preceding chapter; its futility is further indicated by the discovery of still older manuscripts of the New Testament, notably the Chester Beatty papyri.

Another exception is the translation of the New Testament made by Professor Moffatt, who translated the Greek text of von Soden. This Greek text is somewhat closer to the old King James type than any other of recent vintage; von Soden's faulty method has led gradually to the repudiation of his Greek text by the world of scholarship, and it is not used for scholarly purposes today.

A third exception is the Westminster Version. This was begun by Roman Catholic scholars in 1928 as "A New Translation from the Greek and Hebrew Texts." It makes no statement as to what text is used as the basis of the translation, but it differs from Westcott and Hort, e.g., in the inclusion of Matt.

16:2–3, of the words "Son of God" in Mark 1:1, of the long ending of Mark, and of the interpolations at the end of Luke.

In the Old Testament the variation between the several modern translations is much higher than is the case in the New Testament. This is due to two factors, both growing out of the large number of obscure passages in the extant Hebrew text of the Old Testament. Translators vary in the positions they take (1) as to the number of conjectural emendations which should be accepted and translated and (2) as to the extent to which the evidence of the ancient versions should be used to correct and illuminate the Hebrew text. The American Revised Version, for example, is quite close, almost slavishly close, to the Hebrew text. Theological students have discovered this and use this version as a "help" in translation courses in Hebrew. Several of the modern-speech translations have used the ancient versions, notably the Septuagint, in a number of passages where the Hebrew is meaningless or obviously corrupt. For example, the first edition of the American Translation of the Old Testament printed at the end of the work a list of passages in which the reading of the Septuagint had been preferred to that of the Hebrew.

c) DIFFICULTIES IN BIBLE TRANSLATION

The scholar who works on the translation of the Bible has to overcome some difficulties which are not faced by any and all translators. Thus, in the Old Testament, he faces the special difficulty of the vowelless character of the Hebrew original. This made mistakes in translation almost inevitable. Suppose, Gentle Reader, that you were faced with the task of translating vowelless English into some other language. What, for example, would you make of the following?

PRSDNTGRFLDSLDNSPPRSSFRRPTDNFRTN

This might be "President Garfield sold newspaper issue for reputed new fortune," or "pursued, N. T. Ogriflud sailed, newspapers say, for Europe today on Fauretania."

It is no wonder that translators of the Old Testament have made mistakes in translation. Some of these were made as far back as the first translation of the Old Testament. In the Hebrew of Gen. 47:31 we read, "Jacob leaned back on the head of his bed." In the Septuagint translation of this into Greek, we read, "Jacob bowed upon the head of his staff." The Hebrew for "the bed" as written without vowels is *Hmmtth;* "the staff" is identical, the difference appearing entirely in the vowels. "The bed" is *Hammittah;* "the staff" is *Hammatteh.* The possibilities of confusion in the translating of the vowelless text are obvious. Interestingly enough, the author of the Epistle to the Hebrews quotes the passage with the word "staff," for he used the Septuagint version and not the Hebrew. Thus the modern Bible contains both readings of the word: "bed" in Gen. 47:31 and "staff" in Heb. 11:21.

Another example of the difficulty caused by the

vowelless character of the Hebrew text is found in Jer. 2:23. Our Hebrew text contains a phrase which is now commonly read as "[thou art] a swift dromedary traversing her ways." But the Septuagint translators, working on the same text, supplied a different set of vowels, with the result that their version read, "Her voice cried traversing her ways."

Since the translator of the Bible is translating an ancient document, he faces all the problems raised by the translation of a document from a different culture. Weights and measures, coins, measures of time, the names of days and months, official titles, and dozens of technical terms face the translator with the challenge, "Will you translate us or transliterate?"

Transliteration is the easier and (from one point of view) the more accurate method; but all will agree that it is not the more luminous solution of the task. The reader who learns that the water jars at Cana held two or three metretes apiece has not learned much until someone tells him what a metretes is. If there is to be any translation of measures, it should certainly be into contemporaneous measures. The average American gains little information from the statement of the American Revised Version that the waterpots held two or three "firkins" apiece. Since a large part of the significance of the miracle is the lavish fashion in which the wine was bestowed by Jesus, it is important that the reader should know that each jar held twenty to thirty gallons.

In other of these areas it is harder to set up a rule.

Are the modern equivalents really equivalent? Does the word "church" adequately represent the Pauline *ekklesia?* The translator's mastery of English idiom should ideally be equal to his knowledge of Hebrew or Greek idiom. That this is ever the case is doubtful, but it is not always realized that the deficiency exists as often in knowledge of English as of the original languages. The translator should see the English language as objectively as he sees the Greek or Hebrew; he should be able to estimate accurately the extent to which his English phrases will produce effects equivalent to the effects produced by the language of the original. For the ideal of fidelity in translation includes the preservation of those qualities of the original which determined its effect upon its first readers.

PROGRESS IN TRANSLATION

Although the translators of the Bible face such manifold problems, they have made significant progress. At times this progress has been made possible by the discovery of better texts to translate. We have already noted that it was increased knowledge of the manuscripts that led to the making of the English Revised Version. The great advantage which the Revised Versions—English and American—hold over the King James Version springs from the increased accuracy of the Hebrew and Greek texts which they translated. The repudiation of the Greek text of the New Testament which lies behind the King James Version has been absolute. In the study of the Greek

New Testament in our denominational seminaries and graduate schools, it is nowhere in use today.

Again, the translators of the Bible have been helped from time to time by increased knowledge of the original languages of the Bible. The Renaissance made its contribution to the improvement of the English versions by turning the spotlight on Greek and Hebrew, by developing the study of ancient languages and manuscripts, and by sending scholars back past the Latin translations made in the medieval period to the original languages of ancient documents. By A.D. 1516, both the Hebrew text of the Old Testament and the Greek text of the New Testament had been printed. Translators now turned in increasing numbers to these languages and away from the Latin Vulgate. The ultimate gain in the accuracy of the text translated and the quality of the translation cannot be overemphasized.

Although the centuries that followed A.D. 1516 saw the Greek New Testament studied as well as translated, they often saw the students bewildered by the peculiarities of the Greek in which the New Testament was written. It was early noted that in vocabulary and usage it was a very different language from that in which the great writers of ancient Greece produced their masterpieces. The new and strange words bothered the translators; so, also, did the "unusual" constructions. A study of the sources of New Testament Greek printed as late as 1895 contains a somewhat padded list of five hundred and fifty "biblical" words—words found only in the New

Testament or in the Greek Old Testament. These once-only words, or New-Testament-only words, very naturally baffled the translators. For, while the high-school Sophomore believes that the way to find the meaning of a word is to look in a vocabulary or lexicon, the more advanced student knows that the maker of the lexicon has nothing reliable to put in until he has a reasonable number of occurrences of the word.

Lack of comparable material is equally embarrassing to the man who writes the grammar. If a certain preposition always meant "into" when used with a certain case in the Greek of the fifth century B.C., must it be translated that way in the New Testament in passages where that meaning seemed unsuitable? In the earlier Greek, one preposition meant "concerning" when used with the genitive case; a similar one meant "on behalf of." Should each occurrence in the New Testament be translated in accordance with this usage? For users of the "proof-text" method of Bible study, the doctrine of the atonement hung on the answer. But the scholar can give a definite answer only on the basis of adequate contemporary parallels.

Toward the end of the nineteenth century, a German pastor, Adolf Deissmann, read a publication of some private papers written in Greek in the Roman period and dug up by archeologists working in Egypt. As he read, he was constantly reminded of the vocabulary and construction of the Greek Bible, both in the Septuagint version of the Old Testament and also in the New Testament. With aroused curiosity and increased interest, he made a serious study of the language of these papyri (Egyptian papers) to see what light would be thrown upon the idiom of the Greek Bible. The result has revolutionized the linguistic study of both Greek Testaments, for he first convinced himself and then the world of scholarship that the "biblical" Greek was essentially the Greek in which these nonliterary documents were written.

That Greek was a simple language, the conversational language of ordinary people. In it the farmer's tax receipt was written; in it petitions were sent to Roman officials. Its vocabulary supplied the missing parallels to the long list of New Testament words, until the number now without parallel has been reduced to considerably less than fifty. Even to those words that were already known, increased clarity and significance have come from their appearance in these contemporary documents. The New Testament exhortation to be reconciled to God gains meaning for the student when he hears a dissolute youth away from home implore his mother in a letter, "Be reconciled to me!"

The illumination cast by the study of these documents upon the problems of New Testament grammar has been as helpful as that shed on the meaning of words. The anomalies, the "exceptions" to classical rules, have become regular in our increased knowledge of the Greek of the New Testament period. Many a construction which baffled the student in the days before Deissmann's discovery now became normal and luminous. In view of all this it is not strange that grammars and lexicons of the Greek New Testament have been remade in a flood of new editions since 1900.

All this had tremendous significance for the translation of the New Testament and, indirectly, for that of the Old Testament too. For the first time scholars knew in what kind of language the original New Testament was written. Now it was possible to translate it into an English approximately equivalent in cultural level to the language of the original. Moreover, the translator now knew the meaning of the original much more clearly than his predecessors had done. The result has been a flood of modern-speech translations, which render the New Testament in English of a nonliterary level analogous to that of the Greek original.

The vast majority of these are new translations, not revisions of older translations. Their advance upon earlier translations was made possible by an increase in linguistic knowledge—not by an increase in the accuracy of the Greek and Hebrew texts such as called forth the revised versions of 1881 and 1901. Their excellencies are greater clarity of language, more contemporary language, and a more accurate representation of the language of the original. To compare these translations—at least in the New Testament—with the stately flow of the Tudor translations, as though these more recent translators were striving to match that diction, is a serious error. They must be measured against the original. That many devout persons would today prefer that the New Testament should have been written in a literary Greek cannot alter the fact that it was not. Those whose primary demand upon a version is fidelity will welcome these attempts to take the English reader back into the very quality of the original language.

This is not to argue that such translations as those of Goodspeed and Moffatt are the final word in English versions of the New Testament, or that Moffatt or the makers of the "American Translation" of the Old Testament have translated the Hebrew Scriptures for the last time. On the contrary, it is to be hoped that within fifty years all these translations will either be remade or vanish, so that the path leading to the making of contemporary translations for our children's generation may be free from the obstacles raised by emotional attachments to these present versions.

BIBLIOGRAPHY ON TRANSLATION

GENERAL

SAVORY, THEODORE. *The Art of Translation*. London: Cape, 1957.
  Discusses translation in general terms, and devotes separate chapters to specific subject matters including the classics, poetry, and the Bible.

GOODSPEED, E. J. *The Making of the English New Testament.* Chicago: University of Chicago Press, 1925.
  A history of the making of English versions from 1525 to 1925.

ROBINSON, H. WHEELER (ed.). *The Bible in Its Ancient and English Versions*. Oxford: Clarendon Press, 1940.
  Covers Hebrew, Greek, Syriac, Latin, and English versions.

GRANT, FREDERICK C. *Translating the Bible*. Greenwich: Seabury Press, 1961.

This is both a history of translation and an interesting discussion of translation.

PRICE, I. M. *The Ancestry of Our English Bible* (rev. by W. A. IRWIN and ALLEN WIKGREN). New York: Harper & Row, 1949.

Especially chapters xix–xxvi. Good bibliography.

BRUCE, F. F. *The English Bible: A History of Translations*. New York: Oxford University Press, 1961.

The author describes and evaluates translations from the earliest English translations to the New English Bible, covering twenty-five translations made since 1900. The evaluations are least dependable in regard to the most recent work.

BROWER, REUBEN A. (ed.). *On Translation* ("Harvard Studies in Comparative Literature"). Cambridge, Mass.: Harvard University Press, 1959.

Contains a valuable chapter by Eugene Nida on translating the Bible, with more general discussion of the task of translation in the contemporary world.

TRANSLATIONS[1]

The Revised Standard Version. The title-page reads: *The Holy Bible containing the Old and New Testaments: Revised Standard Version: Translated from the Original Tongues: Being the Version set forth A.D. 1611: Revised A.D. 1881–1885 and A.D. 1901: Compared with the most ancient authorities: and revised A.D. 1952.* New York: Nelson, 1952.

The standard English translation for American Protestant churches. Accurate enough for serious study, idiomatic enough for intelligent reading. The Oxford University Press published it in 1962 as *The Oxford Annotated Bible* with notes and valuable helps for students edited by Herbert G. May and Bruce M. Metzger.

SMITH, J. M. P., and GOODSPEED, EDGAR J. (eds.). *The Bible: An American Translation*. Chicago: University of Chicago Press.

The New Testament was translated from the Westcott and Hort text by Goodspeed in 1923; the Old Testament was translated by A. R. Gor-

---

[1] The more popular and the better modern translations are listed here.

don, T. J. Meek, J. M. Powis Smith, and Leroy Waterman (ed. by
J. M. P. Smith) in 1927. A translation of enduring quality based on the
best texts.

The New English Bible: New Testament. Oxford and Cambridge:
At the University Presses, 1961.

This is a new translation, not a revision, sponsored jointly by Protestant churches in England, Scotland, and Ireland. It is uneven in quality
from book to book, puts a high premium on English style, indulges in
rather free paraphrase, and does not translate a better text than the Revised Versions did.

PHILLIPS, J. B. *The New Testament in Modern English.* New
York: Macmillan, 1958.

This claims to be a translation which uses paraphrase only where necessary for intelligibility. Phillips does not identify the text he translated,
nor can it be identified with any modern scholarly edition. His translation
is vivid and dramatic and colloquial, even where the New Testament is
not. The Epistles are the best part of the work.

KNOX, RONALD A. *The Holy Bible;* a translation from the Latin
Vulgate in the light of the Hebrew and Greek originals.
Authorized by the Hierarchy of England and Wales and the
Hierarchy of Scotland. New York: Sheed & Ward, 1956.

CONFRATERNITY OF CHRISTIAN DOCTRINE. *The Holy Bible.* This
translation by the Episcopal Committee of the Confraternity
of Christian Doctrine is still in progress. The New Testament
was published in 1941. Genesis was published in 1948 and the
translation of the Old Testament has continued since that
date. Complete Bibles are published by combining the new
Confraternity and the older Douai-Challoner versions. As
additional books are translated, the new translation is substituted for the old. There are a number of publishers.

*The Holy Scriptures According to the Massoretic Text: A New
Translation.* Philadelphia: Jewish Publication Society of
America, 1917, reprinted 1955 ff.

A scholarly and stimulating version of the Old Testament.

ORLINSKY, HARRY M. (ed.). *The Torah* (Prophets and Writings
in process). Philadelphia: Jewish Publication Society of America, 1962.

A fresh translation, not a revision.

TRANSLATOR'S TOOLS

TEXTS

For Greek and Hebrew texts see bibliography for chap. ii.

GRAMMARS

a) FOR THE BEGINNER

MOULTON, J. H. *An Introduction to the Study of New Testament Greek* (4th ed. rev.). London: Epworth Press, 1952.

With this is bound "A First Reader in New Testament Greek." A fine introduction with comprehensive treatment of forms and sound introduction to syntax.

COLWELL, E. C., and TUNE, E. W. *A Beginner's Reader-Grammar for New Testament Greek*. New York: Harper & Row, in press for autumn 1964 publication.

A simplified approach to study of forms, with an extensive graded reader.

SELLERS, O. R., and VOIGT, E. E. *Biblical Hebrew for Beginners*. Chicago: Blessing Book Store, 1951.

NAKARAI, T. W. *Biblical Hebrew*. Philadelphia: Maurice Jacobs Press, 1951.

b) FOR THE SPECIALIST

MOULTON, J. H., and HOWARD, W. F. *A Grammar of New Testament Greek*. 3 vols. Edinburgh: T. & T. Clark, 1908–63.

Vol. I is a most stimulating general introduction. Vol. II discusses accidence and word formation. Vol. III, *Syntax*, is by Nigel Turner.

BLASS, F., and DEBRUNNER, A. *A Greek Grammar of the New Testament and Other Early Christian Literature* (trans. and rev. by ROBERT W. FUNK). Chicago: University of Chicago Press, 1961.

The best reference grammar for the syntax of the New Testament.

MAYSER, E. *Grammatik der griechischen Papyri aus der Ptolemäerzeit mit Einschluss der gleichzeitigen Ostraka und der in Ägypten verfassten Inschriften*. Berlin and Leipzig: Walter de Gruyter & Co., 1923——.

An invaluable work for the student of biblical Greek in either Testament. Now being revised and continued.

Gesenius' *Hebrew Grammar*, as edited and enlarged by the late E. Kautzsch (2d English ed. revised in accordance with the 28th German edition [1909] by A. E. Cowley, with a facsimile of the Silvan inscription by J. Euting, and a table of alphabets by M. Ledzbarski). Oxford: Clarendon Press, 1910.

Sperber, A. *A Historical Grammar of Biblical Hebrew* (in preparation).

An exhaustive advanced study of the major problems and suggested solutions.

Rosenthal, Franz. *A Grammar of Biblical Aramaic* ("Porta linguarum Orientalium"). Wiesbaden: Harrassowitz, 1961.

LEXICONS

Brown, F., Driver, S. R., and Briggs, C. *A Hebrew and English Lexicon of the Old Testament: Edited with Constant Reference to the Thesaurus of Gesenius, as Completed by E. Rödiger, and with Authorized Use of the Latest German Editions of Gesenius Handwörterbuch*. Boston: Houghton Mifflin, 1960.

Bauer, Walter. *A Greek-English Lexicon of the New Testament and Other Early Christian Literature* (trans. from the 4th German ed. by William F. Arndt and F. Wilbur Gingrich). Chicago: University of Chicago Press, 1957.

Best Greek-English lexicon.

Moulton, J. H., and Milligan, G. *The Vocabulary of the Greek Testament Illustrated from the Papyri and other Non-literary Sources*. London: Hodder & Stoughton, 1914–29.

A stimulating work, unsurpassed in its field.

Preisigke, F. *Wörterbuch der griechischen Papyrusurkunden* (finished by E. Kiessling). Berlin: Privately printed, 1925–31.

Liddell, H. G., and Scott, R. *A Greek-English Lexicon* (new ed. by H. S. Jones and R. McKenzie). Oxford: Clarendon Press, 1940.

The new edition is a thoroughly revised and augmented edition, down to A.D. 600 but excluding the Church Fathers.

LAMPE, G. W. H. *A Patristic Greek Lexicon.* Oxford: Clarendon Press, 1961——.

Three fascicles have appeared (1963). Christian authors from the Apostolic Fathers to A.D. 800.

CONCORDANCES

LISOWSKY, G. (ed.). *Konkordanz zum hebräischen Alten Testament.* Stuttgart: Privilegierte Württembergische Bibelanstalt, 1958.

HATCH, E., and REDPATH, H. A. *A Concordance to the Septuagint and the Other Greek Versions of the Old Testament Including the Apocryphal Books.* Oxford: Clarendon Press, 1897.

MOULTON, W. F., and GEDEN, A. S. *A Concordance to the Greek Testament, according to the Texts of Westcott and Hort, Tischendorf and the English Revisers.* New York: Scribner's, 1897.

Chapter IV

The Interpretation of the Bible
The Modernizing Method

✿

THE selection and collection of books and the making of a careful translation from an accurate text—all of this merely paves the way to the ultimate question, "What does the Bible mean?" All the minute and tedious studies of language and manuscripts that enter into the study of any ancient literature look ahead to the illumination of the content of that literature; their aim is to make it easier for the modern reader who does not possess technical knowledge to understand the message of these books written long ago in a strange world.

The early Protestant ideal was often so expressed as to suggest that, if the Bible were placed in the hands of the layman in a vernacular translation, there would be no further difficulty. The reader would be his own interpreter. Several centuries of experience have indicated that the untrained layman is often helpless, or too ingenious, as an interpreter of Holy Writ. There was something dismaying about the zeal with which he found the Roman pope indicated by the number "666" in Revelation; and who that has seen it can ever forget the rapt expression of the interpreter who found the explanation of the Beast of Revelation in the N.R.A.?

These extravagances of interpretation—common as they are—are no excuse for withholding the Bible from the people or for prescribing an "orthodox" interpretation with ecclesiastical sanctions. The solution lies in a clear grasp of what is involved in interpretation of the Bible. Such a grasp can be attained by those who are in no sense experts; all that it demands are (1) a study of the problems and methods of interpretation and (2) a willingness to accept the results of the experts' work in the light of that study. This volume on the study of the Bible finds its goal in the following discussion of the interpretation of the Scriptures. This chapter, with the two following chapters, is primarily concerned with the task of finding out the significance of the Bible's content; not that any attempt is made to expound or define all that content but rather that methods of study are classified, criticized, explained, and exemplified.

Generally speaking, there are only two methods of interpreting the Bible. They are the "modernizing" method and the "historical" method. Each of these methods has numerous modifications and forms, but these two are separated from each other by a gulf that is so wide that it dwarfs all the minor divisions. The method which has been called the modernizing method has its feet firmly planted in the period in which the interpreter lives; it finds the Bible's basic meaning with reference to the "modern" period in which the

interpreter is, naturally, most interested. The historical method, on the other hand, finds the Bible's
basic meaning with reference to the situation in which
the Bible was written.

THE MODERNIZING METHOD DEFINED

The interpreter who uses this method approaches
the Bible with certain answers already in his possession. His basic assumption is that what was written
by a Hebrew prophet in the eighth century B.C. or by
a Christian missionary in A.D. 50 finds its significance
in the interpreter's day. The forces that lead to this
emphasis upon the interpreter's own group can be
easily identified and understood. The basis upon
which this type of interpretation rests is the canonization of the Scriptures. As soon as any scripture is
recognized as authoritative in the cult, leaders of the
religious group are forced to come to terms with it.
In succeeding generations the appeal to this authority
from the past becomes more difficult. The leaders
with new programs must either repudiate the Bible
and set up some substitute or they must forcefully
interpret the Scriptures into agreement with the new
program and the new needs. One can easily understand that, in spite of the number of laws canonized
in the Pentateuch (613 according to one count),
the changes that came with the centuries would
inevitably produce problems. No matter how exactly
these laws fitted the situations in which they were
produced, there was bound to be some little strain in
applying them to a later situation. Unfortunately,

the doctrine that they were God's law grew in rigor of definition as time passed. A modernizing interpretation is an almost inevitable result of the canonization of the Scriptures as the full and complete revelation of God's will.

The simple syllogisms employed by the modernizing interpreter are something like this. The will of God for his people is fully and adequately expressed in Scripture. We are God's people. Therefore, God's will for us is expressed in the Scriptures. If the interpreter is a legalist, he reasons as follows: God's word contains his divine law for his people; we are his people; therefore, we will find divine law for our guidance in the Bible. If he is primarily interested in the end of the world, he arrives at similar conclusions. God would not fail to tell his people (us) when the world was to end; therefore, we can find in the Bible the date of the end.

This type of interpretation owes most of its worst features to dogmas about the Bible as the Word of God. Since all Scripture is the Word of God, there can be no contradictions in it. Since all Scripture is the Word of God, it can have nothing superfluous in it. Since Scripture is the Word of God, it can contain nothing unworthy of God. Each of these dogmas leads to the perversion and the modernizing of Scripture.

To take up the last one first—it plainly means that the Bible cannot say anything which the interpreter regards as unworthy of God. But this can be a sound rule for interpretation only if the interpreter's ideas as to what is worthy of God coincide identically with all the biblical author's ideas—or with God's own thoughts. Unless the student is willing to make these assumptions, he should avoid interpretations based on this dogma. In practice the appeal to this dogma gives the interpreter license to edit Scripture into conformity with his own ideas.

The insistence that the Scripture can have nothing superfluous is another screen for modernizing interpretation. The perversion is justified by a question-begging argument. Anything that does not apply to the interpreter's own day is labeled superfluous; therefore, it must be made to apply to the interpreter's times. To the Gentile Christians of the first few centuries the food laws of the Pentateuch were superfluous if taken in their natural meaning. This was enough to convince almost every one of the early Christian interpreters of the Old Testament that these laws were not to be taken in their literal meaning. They must have some Christian meaning, some modern meaning. Thus Barnabas found that the proscription of animals that do not chew the cud is an exhortation to meditation. Moreover, he felt sure that this was the primary and original intention of the law.

In the fourteenth chapter of Genesis, the reader is informed that Abraham defeated the invading kings with an army composed of three hundred and eighteen men born in his own house. Later interpreters of this passage, both Jewish and Christian, found little religious inspiration in this statement of fact. They, therefore, searched for some deeper meaning. The number "318" suggested that a modern meaning might be found by the use of numerology. Among both Hebrews and Greeks, letters were used as numbers; that is, all letters had numerical value. From this fact it was easy to find significance in numbers. A Jewish interpreter of this passage, seeking diligently for some significance in it, noticed that Abraham had a servant born in his household named Eliezer (Gen. 15:2–3). The letters in the word Eliezer when added up as numbers total 318. This shows that Abraham's army consisted of Eliezer.

The Christian author of the Letter òf Barnabas felt sure that the Old Testament was written for the sake of the Christians. But what did the Christians care about how many servants Abraham had who were born in his own household? They were not interested in the number of his servants. Yet this statement must mean something to them otherwise this line of Scripture would be superfluous, and the Word of God could not contain anything superfluous. By the ingenious application of a little numerology, Barnabas was able to find in this verse a prediction that Jesus was to be crucified.

For it says, "And Abraham circumcised from his household eighteen men and three hundred." What then was the knowledge that was given him? Observe that he first says the eighteen, and after a pause the three hundred. The eighteen is I, ten, and H, eight; you have Jesus [IHSOUS]. And because the cross was to have grace in the Tau [Tau, T, equals 300], he says also the three hundred. He indicates, then, Jesus in the two letters; and in the one, the cross. He who freely planted his teaching within us knows this. No one has learned a more excellent lesson from me, but I know that you are worthy [ix. 8–9].

An implication of this modernizing method of interpretation is that the first readers of the Scripture could not understand it. When the Scofield Reference Bible says that the mention of Rosh, Meshek, and Tubal in Ezek. 38:2–3 means Russia, Moscow, and Tbolsk, "in the opinion of all interpreters [!]," it asks us to believe that the first readers of Ezekiel (and their successors for a thousand years) could not possibly understand what Ezekiel was talking about. One wonders why God was so concerned about the generation which was to read the Scofield Bible and so little concerned with Ezekiel's contemporaries. Early Christian interpreters did not shrink from the implications of this type of exegesis. Justin Martyr denied that the literal meaning of the Old Testament had any significance; Barnabas indignantly denies that the Old Testament is the joint possession of Jew and Christian. He insists that it belongs to the Christians alone. Since it was written for the Christians, the Jews naturally could not understand it.

TYPES OF MODERNIZING INTERPRETATION

A rich vocabulary has grown up around the effort to read modern meanings into the Scriptures. Exponents of this school of interpretation speak of the use of allegory, typology, numerology, tropology, and the anagogical sense. The distinction between these various systems, or methods, or senses, is not always clear to the naked eye.

As an example of the lack of definite meaning in these sonorous terms, consider the distinctions made between the allegorical meaning, the tropological meaning, and the anagogical meaning of Scripture, as a contemporary manual on the study of the Bible presents them. By way of preface, we should note that the author insists on the existence of a literal meaning in addition to these "spiritual" or "mystical" meanings.

The allegorical meaning is the reference of the text to a doctrine of the faith, especially to Christ and the church. If the text "admits or requires" this reference, then it possesses an allegorical meaning; e.g., Matt. 12:39 shows that the experience of Jonah with the sea monster refers allegorically to the resurrection of Jesus.

The tropological meaning of a passage is the application of a passage to moral life. In Gen. 15:6 we read that Abraham believed, and it was reckoned to him for righteousness. In Rom. 4:23 Paul finds here the meaning that mankind should believe in Christ.

The anagogical meaning of a passage is the application that it allows to the future life. The familiar story of Noah and the ark in Genesis may be applied also to the faithful who find salvation in the church (cf. Matt. 24:37; I Pet. 3:20).

The reader can easily see that there is no distinction of method here; these labels are used for one method with the results classified according to their subject matter. Even this classification does not seem very objective to judge from the author's own examples; for the definition of the first class would include the examples of the second and third classes. Allegory, tropology, typology, anagoge, and their brood are basically one type of interpretation. On the assumption that there is a deeper meaning in Scripture than has been expressed by the inspired writer, these interpreters proceed in any devious way, on the basis of hints which first win their significance in the interpreters' own eyes.

One of the few "methods" of modernizing the meaning of Scripture which can be recognized as a distinct pattern of interpretation is numerology. This rests on the numerical values of the Hebrew and Greek alphabets and makes much of the fact that it works on the original languages of the Bible. We have already noted a glowing example of its use in antiquity in Barnabas' explanation of the number "318."

Not only does numerology make it possible to find a modern meaning in a dark passage but it also demonstrates that the Scripture is the Word of God. Three and seven are good numbers. God made the natural world with its seven planets, seven tones in the scale, seven colors, etc.; the Bible is full of sevens; therefore, God wrote the Bible. The number of nouns in certain verses of Genesis, chapter 1, is a multiple of seven. If nouns don't work out, adjectives, adverbs, or prepositions will. It is here that the subjective element enters. The interpreter selects the units to be counted or the words to be translated into their numerical equivalents.

The same methods will prove the inspiration of any document. I applied it some years ago to the letter of Ignatius to the Ephesians and unearthed an enormous mass of threes and sevens. A hurried count of the first paragraph of the popular novel *Gone with the Wind* showed that the first sentence had twenty-one words, three 7's; the second, twenty-eight words or four 7's. Add these together and you get seven 7's. The third sentence has three nouns. The first paragraph has twenty-eight (4×7) nouns, seven proper adjectives, and nine (3×3) adverbs. Will some numerologist claim inspiration for this book? No, he will not; for numerology proves the divine origin of the Bible only to those who knew it in advance.

It might be possible to separate typology, tropology, etc., from allegory—if we were using these terms for the first time today. But they have a long history—a history in which they are often confused with one another. At first, the interpreters spoke of only one meaning above the literal meaning. This was usually referred to as a "spiritual" meaning. When skilful exegetes like Origen found three meanings, they were driven to poetry for labels and definitions of the extra meanings. Augustine found four meanings in a passage, and the later ages produced as many as seven meanings from one passage, although the classification is stretched somewhat thin at spots.

In Paul's interpretation of Abraham's family life

we have a clear example of a confusion in terminology which began early and still persists. In Gal. 4:21-31 he presents Sarah and Hagar, Isaac and Ishmael, as types of Judaism and Christianity. The reader's natural inclination is to classify this as typological interpretation; but in 4:24 Paul says that these Scripture texts are allegorical. Of all the titles used for these modernizing methods, allegorical is the most fitting. Its basic significance of saying one thing and meaning another is at home with these interpreters.

MODERNIZED BIBLES

A sounder classification of the modernizing schools of interpretation can be based on the messages they read into the Scriptures. Each of these interpreters brings a certain message to the Bible and reads it into the sacred text by means of his system of interpretation. But not all of them bring the same message to the Book.

The Jewish rabbis, for example, in the days after their national glory had departed, brought to the Torah a glorification of the scribe and his work which the sacred book had not known before. The extent to which this was done has often been illustrated, but no more forceful example can be found than the Targum on the Song of Deborah. This is not designed primarily as interpretation but rather as translation; however, we have seen in the chapter on translation that the two are not always as distinct as they should be. Judg. 5:8-9 is a strong statement of the lack of soldiers in Israel; the Targum expands this into a wordy praise of the scribes who interpreted the Law accurately and patiently in the days of crisis.

The Christians of the first few centuries brought to the Old Testament a belief that Jesus was the Messiah; this belief they read into almost every line of the Jewish Scriptures. Two of the great classics in this "interpretation" are *The Letter of Barnabas* and Justin's *Dialogue with Trypho*.

We have already seen the nature of the interpretation in Barnabas, where "318" predicts the crucifixion of Jesus; Justin is no more restrained. For example, he quotes (from the Greek Old Testament) Exod. 20:22; 23:20, 21, in which God tells Moses to announce to the people, "I send my angel before you to guard you on the way, and to bring you into the land which I have prepared for you. Hark unto him and obey him, do not resist him; for he will not withhold [punishment] from you, for my name is upon him." Who is this guide? asked Justin. Who else but Jesus (the Greek form of Joshua!)—*Dialogue* lxxv. 1.

Justin finds the cross (*Dialogue* lxxxvi) in the "tree" of life planted in Paradise, in the "rod" with which Moses was sent to free Israel, in the "tree" cast into the bitter waters of Mara, in the "rods" used by Jacob to win his uncle's sheep, in the "staff" with which, as Jacob "boasted," he had crossed the Jordan, in the "ladder" of Jacob's dream upon which he saw God— not the Father—"fixed," in the "rod" of Aaron which blossomed, in the "shoot" from the root of Jesse which Isaiah predicted, in David's portrayal of the righteous man as a "tree" planted by the water courses, in David's claim that the righteous would flourish like a palm "tree," in the "tree" from which God appeared to Abraham—the oak of Mambre—in the seventy willow "trees" which the people found when they crossed over Jordan, in the comforting "rod" and "staff" of the twenty-third Psalm, in the "tree" [ax handle] which Elisha threw into the Jordan to recover the lost ax head, in the "staff" which Judah gave Tamar as a pledge for the payment of her prostitution.

These are selections from only two, albeit a striking two, out of scores of Christian interpreters who modernized the Jewish Bible into a Christian book. With a few exceptions, early Christian interpreters ignored the great messages of the inspired prophets and poets of Israel except where they could be transformed into messianic texts. Their guiding principles were expressed by Augustine in a memorable couplet: "The New Testament in the Old is latent; the Old Testament in the New is patent." One result of this is the impoverishment of the Christian tradition, which has slighted the prophets' burning attacks on injustice, greed, and exploitation of the poor to concentrate its attention on fantastic "predictions" of the cross.

Other times, other Bibles. Once the Christian-messianic nature of the Old Testament was accepted by all but the Jews, the church brought different messages to be read into the Bible. For example, Clement of Alexandria was worried by the effeminacy of some of the Christians of his day. One of their perverted habits was that of shaving. Imagine his horror when he found large numbers of Christian men shaving off not merely part of the beard (he could have stood that) but every last whisker! Against this contemporary custom, Clement invoked the authority of the Scriptures. He couldn't find a law saying, "Do not shave"; but in the one hundred and thirty-third Psalm brotherly unity is likened to "the precious ointment upon the head, that ran down upon the beard, even Aaron's beard: that went down to the skirts of his garments." David wrote this so that Clement's contemporaries might not shave.

Each generation—often each individual interpreter —brought a new message to the Bible and found it there. In the days of the Reformation, it was Lutheranism, or Calvinism, or Arminianism. German interpreters wrote learned works showing that Adam was a Lutheran. Frenchmen proved that not only Paul but also Jesus and Abraham were faithful to Calvin's *Institutes*.

In this regard the Roman Catholic church differs from the others in the degree of explicitness with which it directs the interpreter to find in the Scriptures the teaching of the church. Its logic is simple. Since these books have a divine origin, written with the aid of the Holy Spirit, they can be understood only with the same divine assistance. But the Holy Spirit cannot be certainly found anywhere except in the church; therefore, the interpreter must first find out the opinion of the church and be guided by it.

The extent of ecclesiastical control over interpretation is plainly stated in an encyclical of Pope Leo XIII, "Providentissimus Deus" (November 18, 1893). After insisting that it is the place of the church to judge the true sense of Scripture, he reassures the interpreter as to the liberty with which he may work. The church in no way hinders the study of the Bible except as it prevents error, he says; for the individual scholar can exercise his liberty in two ways. First, his study of passages not yet officially interpreted by the church may help the church to decide what the correct interpretation is. Second, his work on passages whose meaning has been defined by the church may expound that meaning more clearly or defend it better from hostile attack. The primary object of the Catholic interpreter's work in those areas where the judgment of the church has already been pronounced "is to interpret those passages in that identical sense, and to prove by all the resources of learning that sound laws of interpretation admit of no other meaning." The reader might assume that the Catholic interpreter actually is free in those areas where judgment has not yet been pronounced, but the encyclical goes on to point out that legitimate interpretation is bound to produce meanings in harmony with Catholic doctrines. Any interpretation that finds contradictions in the Scriptures or finds the Scriptures contradicting the teaching of the Roman Catholic church is either "foolish or false."

The justification of ecclesiastical control of interpretation, which is practiced by Protestant churches as well as by the Roman Catholic, is that it prevents error. The wild luxuriance of interpretations made possible by the modernizing method have inevitably embarrassed all cults which rest upon the authority of Scripture. The presence of a large number of conflicting interpretations of the same passage always produces a strain in those areas where orthodoxy is prized. The judgment may be hazarded that uniformity was one of the desires of those who in various times and places have set up cult control of interpretation.

Examples of this painful extravagance in interpretation can be found in the meanings found by Christian scholars in Rev. 13:18—". . . . for it is the number of a man, and his number is six hundred and sixty-six." Irenaeus claimed that the number was Noah's age at the time of the flood plus the height and breadth of the image set up by Nebuchadnezzar; he identified "the man" as Evanthus, or Lateinos, or Titan. For Hippolytus it meant "I deny (my crucified Savior)." To more modern interpreters, it has meant Mohammed, Pope Benedict IX, any pope, Martin Luther, Lenin, the N.R.A., etc. Such a rank growth of definition creates stress within the cult.

This pressure was felt in Judaism in the days of the rabbis. Out of it arose the dictum that no interpretation could be accepted which went against the Tradition, the oral interpretation. This made the Tradition rather than the Scripture the norm. Quite analogous is the Roman Catholic position quoted above—although it must be remembered that Judaism has no monarchical authoritative hierarchy.

The Protestant churches have followed similar practices although to a less degree. The primitive freedom of the individual interpreter was soon curbed by the formulation of authoritative confessions of faith, or articles of religion. The doctrines championed in these confessions are defined as an accurate statement of the meaning of Scripture. This promulgation limited the freedom of the interpreter who desired to be orthodox, for it prescribed certain interpretations as the correct interpretations and anathematized others. Thus both British and Continental scholars of the Reformation period in their interpretation of the Apocalypse abstained from the millennial views of earlier scholars whose work they accepted, for the Augsburg and Helvetic confessions had branded Chiliasm as a heresy.

The situation of the layman whose Scripture is modernized for him by the church lacks the confusion of freer believers. He often welcomes the increased surety even when it is purchased at the cost of freedom. The value to the institutionalists in the cult of admitting only those modernizations which they favor is unquestioned. But it is the belief of modern scholarship that there is a better way. The history of the Christian world has failed to convince most students of history that errors can be avoided in any field of study by the exercise of ecclesiastical authority. Progress in modern learning has followed —not preceded—the emancipation of scholarship from ecclesiastical shackles.

BIBLIOGRAPHY ON INTERPRETATION

GENERAL

BRIGGS, CHARLES AUGUSTUS. *General Introduction to the Study of Holy Scripture*. New York: Scribners, 1899.

Chapter 11, pp. 247–92, "History of the Higher Criticism of Holy Scripture." Chapter 18, pp. 427–73, "History of the Interpretation of Holy Scripture."

CHARLES, R. H. *Studies in the Apocalypse*. Edinburgh: T. & T. Clark, 1913.

Chapters i and ii give a history of the interpretation of the Book of Revelation.

DANA, H. E. *Searching the Scriptures: A Handbook of New Testament Hermeneutics*. New Orleans: Bible Institute Memorial Press, 1936.

This is written from a conservative viewpoint.

EAKIN, FRANK. *Revaluing Scripture*. New York: Macmillan, 1928.

This work offers a revaluation of the scriptures of all religions as a basis for revaluing the Jewish-Christian Scriptures.

FULLERTON, K. *Prophecy and Authority: A Study in the History of the Doctrine and Interpretation of Scripture*. New York: Macmillan, 1919.

A very readable and stimulating treatment of the problems of interpretation.

GILBERT, G. H. *Interpretation of the Bible: A Short History*. New York: Macmillan, 1908.

The best chronological treatment of interpretation in English today.

———. *Jesus and His Bible*. New York: Macmillan, 1926.

A careful investigation of the methods of interpretation employed by Jesus, with an Appendix on the use of the Old Testament in Paul and Hebrews.

PEAKE, A. S. *The Nature of Scripture*. London: Hodder & Stoughton, 1922.

This deals with modern criticism, its permanent results, the enduring value of Old Testament and New Testament, the evangelical faith, and the modern view of Scripture, etc. A sane and careful study.

ROBINSON, T. H. "The Methods of Higher Criticism," in *The People and the Book*, ed. A. S. PEAKE. Oxford: Clarendon Press, 1925.

Exposition of these methods as applied to parts of the Old Testament.

SEISENBERGER, MICHAEL. *Practical Handbook for the Study of the Bible* (new rev. ed.). New York: Joseph F. Wagner, Inc., 1925.

A Roman Catholic manual published with the imprimatur. It gives English translations of the important papal decrees relating to Scripture (pp. 159–86). Interpretation is discussed in pages 449 ff.

SMITH, H. P. *Essays in Biblical Interpretation*. Boston: Marshall Jones Co., 1921.

Stimulating and valuable discussion of interpretation of the Old Testament.

TRATTNER, E. R. *Unravelling the Book of Books: being the Story of How the Puzzles of the Bible Were Solved and Its Documents Unravelled*. New York: Scribner's, 1929.

An interesting and readable approach to the story of biblical criticism.

ADVANCED

KITTEL, G. *et al. Theologisches Wörterbuch zum Neuen Testament*. Stuttgart: Kohlhammer, 1932——.

Technical studies of important words.

LOOFS, F. *Leitfaden zum Studien der Dogmengeschichte* (4th ed.). Halle a.S., Niemeyer, 1906.

REUSS, EDUARD. *History of the Sacred Scriptures of the New Testament* (trans. from the 5th German ed. by E. L. HOUGHTON). Edinburgh: T. & T. Clark, 1884.

SMITH, H. *Ante-Nicene Exegesis of the Gospels*. 6 vols. New York: Macmillan, 1925.

Quotes this material in order of the scriptural passages in English translation.

Chapter V

The Interpretation of the Bible
The Historical Method
Literary Criticism

✲

THE basic task of interpretation, as the advocates of this method conceive it, is to establish the literal meaning of the sacred text for its first readers. In their insistence on the primacy of the literal meaning they do not deny or slight the poetic and figurative elements in the Scripture but insist that these elements be identified and interpreted according to the literary standards of the age in which they were produced. They do not deny that the Scriptures can have other values today than they have had in the past, but they see the task of defining these modern values as one transcending the field of historical criticism. The task which they assign to the interpreters of the Bible as their own peculiar task in a special discipline is the determination of the meaning of these documents in the time of their origin.

This type of interpretation is essentially an application of the methods of historical study. It strives to be as objective as historical study can be.

It unhesitatingly submits its results to the most searching scholarly examination. It accepts correction and change, for it is supported by no dogma of infallibility. Unlike the modernizing methods described above, it brings no answers to the investigation. It comes with questions and with an eagerness to find the historical evidence which will establish the correct—the intended—meaning of a passage. It is full of hope, for it looks back upon a history of glorious achievement, but it promises no rush deliveries of adequate interpretations

NO DISTINCTIVE TECHNIQUES

But, though it brings no ready-made answers to the study of the Christian literature, it does bring certain convictions as to method and procedure and the significance of evidence—convictions which it shares with those who work in other areas of historical investigation. It assumes that Christianity is a movement like other religious movements; it believes that Christianity like all other religions inherited much, borrowed freely, and was constantly changing its primitive elements and as constantly adapting what it adopted. When it finds two very similar phenomena appearing in the same area at approximately the same time, it assumes the existence of some significant relationship between them. It has learned that hostility between religions does not exclude the influence of one upon the other.

It is convinced that the methods and techniques applied to the solution of problems in the Christian literature must not differ from the methods used in the study of similar problems in other literatures. Take, for example, the problems involved in the miracle stories of the Bible. If the student of the Bible appeals to the general reliability of the biblical writers as guaranty of the accuracy of these stories, he must accept miracle stories from the pagan cults which are related by reliable writers. If the testimony of eyewitnesses is enough to establish the validity of these incidents, pagan miracles attested by eyewitnesses must be accepted also.

The position of the conservative Protestant in regard to miracles is singularly indefensible in its limitation of miracles to those recorded in the Scriptures. This would bring the age of miracles to an end about the middle of the second century, but the Christian writers of the second, third, and fourth centuries are entirely unaware that the age of miracles is over and continue to report the miraculous achievements of Christians until modern times changed the basic world-view.

The Roman historian Tacitus was a writer of more than average dependability and was decidedly against superstition and extravagance. It is significant, therefore, to find him accepting as fact a story of a double miraculous healing. When Vespasian was in Alexandria, a blind man and a cripple appealed to the emperor for healing. The sufferers were advised to make this supplication by Egyptian deities. Vespasian at first demurred but finally yielded to their importunity and healed them by applying his saliva to the eyes of the blind and stepping on the ankle of the cripple. Tacitus assures his readers that he received the story from eyewitnesses after the dynasty of Vespasian had left the throne, when flattery would not create such stories.

The interpreter of Scripture who uses the historical method does not permit himself to use any means of explaining the healing of the lame man at the pool of Bethesda which he cannot use with equal effect to explain the healing by Vespasian in Alexandria.

For the sake of emphasis and clarity, let it be said again that there are no methods of biblical study which are not at the same time methods of studying other religious literatures. This is not to deny that a student may need some particular tool in the study of the Christian Bible which he will not need elsewhere (e.g., a knowledge of biblical Aramaic) but only to insist on the general agreement in matters of importance for methodology between biblical scholarship and the scholarship of the humanities in general. The methods employed in the study of Plato and Plutarch, of Chaucer and Corneille, are also employed in the study of Isaiah and Paul.

We have seen in a preceding chapter the essential oneness in methods of textual criticism, whether the text studied be that of Chaucer, the *Roman de la rose*, or the Bible. In a generation now gone, students of textual criticism in the humanities were under great obligation to two biblical scholars, Westcott and Hort. Today the debt is paid by the work of such eminent scholars as Hunt, Bédier, and Collomp. The methods worked out by Hunt in the study of Greek papyrus texts of the classical authors and by Bédier in the study of the *Lai de l'ombre* are being applied all too tardily to the study of the biblical text.

The plea for some special endowment as a prerequisite for biblical study seems rather out of place in such areas as textual criticism and the study of biblical languages. It is obvious—even to the most dogmatic—that here an ounce of intelligence is worth a pound of piety. But in the field of interpretation there are many to echo the claim advanced by Roman Catholicism: The Bible is an inspired book; it can be understood only with the help of inspiration. The Protestant often makes the same claim with reference to the inspiration of the individual rather than of the church.

The student who uses the historical method of interpreting the Bible relies upon no supernatural aids. What can be known by the conscientious and well-trained student is his objective. This does not include—as he will gladly admit—the proof or disproof of dogmas whose authority inheres in their promulgation by some cult. Yet, however much his appreciation of the message of some inspired author may be increased by the fact that he has had an analogous religious experience, he refuses to impugn the reliability of human intelligence by assenting to the popular fallacy that the messages of the sainted authors can be understood only by those who have duplicated their experiences.

In so far, therefore, as he is a historian, he resolutely rejects all special treatment, all concessions to the cloth; he refuses to use a technique that will not work elsewhere. Yet the number of techniques he calls upon is large. All the resources of literary and historical criticism, the results of philological study, the political, economic, social, and religious background of the books, and the archeologist's spade—all these make their contribution to the understanding of the Scriptures. The techniques which are most familiar to the student in Protestant schools are those which are at home in the field of literary criticism.

LITERARY CRITICISM DEFINED

The tasks faced by the student of the biblical literature have been most memorably grouped in a series of six questions: Who? When? Where? To Whom? Why? What? Authorship, date, place of composition, audience, purpose, and content—these make convenient subdivisions of that literary criticism of the Bible which is frequently referred to under the technical term of "introduction," or, more fully, "introduction to the literature of the Bible." Some of these questions move out of the purely literary realm into that of history, but they have usually been treated with an emphasis on the more purely literary questions.

For example, the question "What?" brings the content or message of the book into investigation. But, when we use it under the heading of literary criticism, we turn most naturally to the literary features of its content. Such purely literary questions as, "Is this book poetry or prose?" raise issues of great importance for the interpreter. Hebrew poetry had rules of composition and structure which differ widely from those used in English versification. An ignorance of the nature of parallelism in the poetic part of the Hebrew Scriptures often has disastrous results in the final interpretation of the passage.

One of the common types of Hebrew parallelism is called "synonymous parallelism"; in it the second line repeats the content and thought of the first with no more than minor modification. In Zech. 9:9, the prophet exhorts Jerusalem in language that is full of this parallelism: "Rejoice greatly, O daughter of Zion; shout, O daughter of Jerusalem: behold, your king comes unto you; he is just, and having salvation; lowly, and riding upon an ass, even upon a colt, the foal of an ass." It is plain that the daughter of Zion is identical with the daughter of Jerusalem and that the colt and the ass are one. But, to the author of Matthew's Gospel, the double mention of the animal implied two animals, and he interprets the fulfilment of the passage with that in mind. Matt. 21:6–7, "And the disciples went and did even as Jesus appointed them, and brought the ass, and the colt, and put *on them* their garments; and he sat *upon them*." An ignorance of a literary form led Matthew to ask us to picture Jesus as riding two animals into Jerusalem.

It needs no such example to persuade the seasoned student of any literature that a knowledge of literary forms and their significance is a prerequisite to adequate interpretation. An awareness of the variation in structure between the Shakespearean and the Italian form of the sonnet is essential to the interpretation of an anthology of English sonnets. It is equally true that the interpreter of apocalypses will be amply rewarded for the time spent in mastering the literary pattern of apocalyptic composition.

a) DATING OF DOCUMENTS

Less obviously literary, but equally a problem faced in the study of any piece of literature, is the problem of date. There is no difference in methods employed in the task of establishing the date of the Gospel of John and the date of the Discourses of Epictetus. In both cases the scholar will assemble all the available evidence, evaluate it as carefully as possible, and thus reach his conclusion as to the date of composition.

For convenience of handling, the evidence is usually assembled under two categories—external and internal. These terms refer to the document itself; that evidence which comes from outside the document is called "external" evidence. Invaluable evidence as to the date of a book is found in quotations from it. The latest possible date for its composition is fixed by the first clear quotation from it in another writing which can be dated. For this evidence to be certain, however, the quotation must be unmistakable, and the date of the document in which the quotation occurs must be established beyond question. Further external evidence for date is to be found in explicit tradition as to the time of composition of a document. There is not much early tradition of this sort as to the date of the books of the Bible. The Christian tradition begins to specify dates for its documents no earlier than the last two décades of the second century.

It is only in the last few years that manuscripts of the Bible have been found which are themselves assigned to dates close enough to the origin of the sacred literature to be of value in the determination of date. In 1935 C. H. Roberts published a fragment of one page of the Fourth Gospel, which he assigned on the basis of its handwriting to the first half of the second century. Several New Testament scholars welcomed the publication of this fragment as evidence that the Fourth Gospel was written before A.D. 100 or at the very latest soon after 100. This conclusion rests on two assumptions; and, since they are assumptions that are frequently made, they deserve criticism.

The first of these assumptions is that the dating of a papyrus document written in a literary hand is accurate within a score of years. One New Testament handbook says of the new John fragment that it was written "about A.D. 130" and then proceeds to argue from the year 130 with as much finality as though this manuscript were actually dated in A.D. 130. In the present state of our knowledge on the paleography of the Greek papyrus book hand, it seems precarious to assign any such document to a period narrower than a century in extent. No undated

manuscript of a book can establish the existence of
the book before or after a definite year.

This fragment of John's Gospel was found in
Middle Egypt. If it was written "about A.D.130,"
the Gospel itself must have been written before 100
if it took the Gospel five years to win prominence in
Ephesus and twenty-five years or more to reach
Middle Egypt. This argument from the length of
time it would take a Christian book to circulate after
publication is commonly employed, although there
are no objective data available to modern scholarship
which would make it possible for us to ascertain the
facts. So far as the speed of communication is concerned, no one assumes that it would take a year to
move a book from Ephesus to Middle Egypt, or from
Alexandria to Rome. Christian travelers made these
distances in less than a year, and it is certainly conceivable that they could have carried a book with
them. As to the length of time it took any particular
book to become known, we have no data. Those
who have observed the spread of books in modern
times might argue that a book is most widely known
right after publication, but arguments from analogy
are dangerous; the safest course for the student is to
reject all arguments as to date that rest on an appeal
to the length of the period essential to the winning
of an audience for a book.

The internal evidence for the date of a document
may include a definite reference to a date. The mention of the fifteenth year of Tiberius Caesar in Luke
3:1 demands a date later than that for the composi-

tion of that Gospel. Isaiah's first vision (6:1 ff.), his
"call to preach," opens with the invaluable date line,
"In the year that King Uzziah died." Even more
valuable are casual or incidental references to events,
persons, or things that can be dated. A medieval
document that casually referred to a trip in an air-
plane could not be medieval no matter how explicitly
it was dated. Chapter 14 of the Book of Genesis tells
of Abraham pursuing Lot's captors far into the north
country "as far as Dan"; this shows that this story
in Genesis was written after the events described in
chapter 18 of Judges, where the tribe of Dan moves
into the north for the first time.

The identification of sources that are dated or
datable sometimes helps in the dating of a document.
The identification of an author whose date is known
leads directly to the dating of the composition that
came from his pen. The place of the literary work in
the history of thought, culture, and social movements
is another indication of date. A Jewish document
which assumes the control of Palestine by Gentiles
cannot be placed in the reign of David. A Christian
book which on every occasion prefixes *homoousion* to
the word Christ cannot come from the first century of
Christian history. Christian documents which assume the authority of ecumenical councils, or the
papacy, or reflect a highly developed monasticism,
etc., are not earlier than A.D. 250. The caliber of the
language itself will often assist in the dating of a
document. The only books in the Hebrew canon
which use Aramaic extensively are assigned late

dates on the basis of both linguistic and non-linguistic evidence. Old Testament scholars refer to the use of late Hebrew as an indication of the date of various passages. No document written in a form of Greek which had lost the infinitive and the optative and possessed an indeclinable participle would ever be accepted as an original composition of the first Christian centuries.

b) AUTHORSHIP OF DOCUMENTS

Another example of the employment of the techniques of literary criticism can be drawn from the study of authorship. The methods employed by students of the Bible are identical with those employed by students of English literature in the evaluation of the claim that Bacon wrote Shakespeare. The external evidence here is of two kinds: the tradition as to authorship and the light thrown on the authorship by the way in which the document was received by its public. Internal evidence of the most value is derived from a study of the vocabulary and style of the document with reference to other works by the author and the comparison of ideas and content.

The most clear-cut decision of a dispute as to the authorship of a biblical book has been won in the case of the Letter to the Hebrews. The question at issue was, "Did the Apostle Paul write this book?" The answer established by several generations of careful scholarly study is an emphatic negative. For purposes of illustration, the arguments and evidence that led to the acceptance of this answer are briefly summarized here.

The external evidence for the Pauline authorship of Hebrews is far from unanimous; in fact, it divides quite cleanly on geographical lines. In the East, as early as Clement of Alexandria, the letter is referred to as Paul's work; although some later leaders support no more than a mediated Pauline authorship i.e., they think that Paul dictated it to a disciple or that it was the work of some ardent Paulinist. In the West the situation is quite different. Tertullian alludes to it as the work of Barnabas, as though that authorship was unquestioned. No leader of the church in the West accepts it as the work of Paul until the time of Hilary of Poitiers, the second half of the fourth century. From the Muratorian canon to Jerome, the Latin church rejects the Pauline authorship. This is the more striking when it is remembered that it is now generally agreed that the letter was written to Rome, and it is certain that Clement of Rome was the first Christian writer to make use of the letter. Thus the tradition of Pauline authorship does not arise, and only slowly wins acceptance, in the territory where the letter was first known.

The internal evidence is overwhelmingly against the theory of Pauline authorship. In language, style, ideas, and situation reflected, it is not Pauline. The contrast of its smooth Greek with the rough style of Pauline letters was noticed by Origen and other Alexandrians. It was this which led them to claim only a mediated Pauline authorship for the letter; they were too much at home in Greek to believe that this could have come from the same pen as the letters of Paul. There are striking differences in vocabulary;

even as characteristic a Pauline phrase as "Christ Jesus" does not occur. The essentially Pauline "in Christ," which occurs even in the one-page letter to Philemon, does not occur in Hebrews. The formulas with which quotations from the Scriptures are introduced consistently differ from Paul's usage.

The differences in ideas and religion are equally striking. There is in Hebrews no justification by faith, no attack on justification by law, no hope for Israel, and no advantage in being an Israelite. No Gentiles concern the author of this letter, and faith is little more than a hope—it lacks the robust mysticism of the Apostle to the Gentiles. Here Christ is portrayed as a priest—a figure that cannot be adequately paralleled from Paul's writings. Sanctification, good works, and obedience are the virtues; marriage is praised as a good thing. There is no contrasted spirit and flesh.

This is a different apostle from the author of Galatians, Romans, Corinthians, Thessalonians, etc.; and he writes for a different situation. The Christianity to which this letter is addressed is later than that of Paul's day. The hope of the second coming is faint; many Christians have died, and yet the great day has not dawned. Attendance at the religious services of the Christians is falling off. There is here no claim of apostolic authority, or of any sort of direct contact with the founder of the cult. The clear statement of Heb. 2:3-4 sets the believers at least one generation farther from Jesus than Paul was: ". . . . How shall we escape if we neglect such a great salvation, which in the beginning was spoken by the Lord [Jesus] and then was confirmed unto us by those who had heard it, to whom God bore witness in signs and wonders and various mighty works and gifts of the Holy Spirit according to his plan." It is hardly conceivable that the author of Galatians could thus confess that he received the gospel from men.

Evidence of this kind (and much of its detail has not been quoted) has convinced scholars that the Letter to the Hebrews did not come from the pen or the mind of the Apostle Paul. The alternative theories as to authorship have little more to commend them than their ingenuity, and general scholarly opinion supports two conclusions: first, the Apostle Paul did not write Hebrews; second, we do not know who did.

Decision as to the authorship of other books in the Bible is made in the same way as this decision that Paul was not the author of Hebrews. Equally definite and clear-cut decisions have been reached in regard to many of the other books. This is true, for example, of the book called by the name of Isaiah. It is generally agreed today that chapters 40 ff. are the work of another man than the author of chapters 1–39. The reference to events of the Exile in 40 ff., the differences in religious ideas, etc., all point to another author. In the case of book after book, similar careful study has led to equally definite conclusions as to authorship, and these conclusions are now part of the common fund of knowledge in the field of biblical study.

But it should not be assumed that the study of authorship is a study of accuracy. No scholar assents to the proposition that composition by an apostle or prophet guarantees the historical accuracy of the events related, or that a work written by a non-apostolic and nonprophetic author is by that fact made unreliable. The question as to the reliability of the events in the Fourth Gospel is not a question as to whether or not the Apostle John wrote it. The Scriptures themselves testify that at least one apostle was unreliable in three statements, and the claim that all who were not apostles or prophets were unreliable needs only to be stated to be rejected.

The importance of identifying the author of these books wherever possible comes from the need of locating them as accurately as we can in place and time. The demonstration that Paul did not write Hebrews does not diminish the historical validity of the letter, but it does make it possible for us to assign it to a definite situation in Rome at the end of the first century. When the letter is read against that background, it becomes luminous with meaning, and the contribution which it makes to our knowledge of early Christianity is more than doubled. The time and energy spent in the accurate determination of authorship by the scholars are, therefore, to be regarded as a preliminary aid to the accurate interpretation of the book, not as attack on, or defense of, traditions as to authorship.

Authorship by apostle or prophet was of tremendous importance to the Christian church in the period of the formation of the canon, as we saw in chapter i; but it has no analogous importance to the modern historian. For purposes of historical study the canon itself can set ño limits. The student cannot assume that what is canonical is accurate and what is apocryphal (noncanonical) is inaccurate. Gospels and Acts that were not in the canon are accepted or rejected by the student on the same bases as those which appear in the canon. Neither apostolic authorship nor canonicity can exempt documents from the most searching investigation of their reliability.

c) IDENTIFICATION OF SOURCES

A fascinating exercise is the identification of sources in some work of literature. The vogue for source analysis of the Scriptures seems to be on the wane at the present moment, but it may not be amiss to point out to the student the tenuous nature of some of the "reconstruction" of literary sources. If no source used by the author in question has survived, and the author does not introduce any sources by formal quotation, the identification of sources is an almost hopeless task unless the author copies his various sources rather slavishly.

For the difficulty of identifying sources is directly proportionate to the literary ability of the author who used the sources. The more he re-wrote and assimilated what he drew from sources, the harder it is to identify the sources in the finished product. A recent evaluation of Elinor Wylie's work quoted one of her sources and compared it with the finished product.

The forty-four lines of the source were reduced to twenty-two in the finished product; at least eight important details were changed by the novelist, and the style of the finished work was the style of Elinor Wylie. The identification of a source so thoroughly re-written as was this one is impossible unless we possess a copy of the source.

Fortunately for the student of biblical documents, their authors were sometimes less rigorous in the rewriting of source material. In the writing of Hebrew history, for example, the method commonly employed in the use of sources was what has been called a "scissors and paste" method. The author copied one section from one source and the next section from another; re-writing was slight in degree and quantity. Very frequently the author refused to choose between his sources and copied the story first from one and then from another.

One of the clearest examples of this can be found in the story of creation in the opening chapters of Genesis. The reader finds the record of creation complete in Gen. 1:1—2:3. In this section, only thirty-four verses in length, creation is finished in six days. God creates by divine fiat day and night, sky, sea and land, plants, stars, sun, moon, animals, birds, and human beings, male and female. The seventh day is hallowed as a day of abstinence from labor. Yet in chapter 2, verse 4, the process of creation starts all over again with the formation of a man for whose sake plants, animals, and a woman are created. The two stories are equally distinct in idea and style. The first is formal in pattern and exalted in tone. In it the work of creation is divided up by days, and a refrain closes the day's work. God creates by the spoken word and, as a climax to his creative activity, hallows the Sabbath by resting on it. In the second story there are no day-by-day divisions; God forms man out of earth, plants a garden, etc. In the first story the deity is consistently referred to as God, in the second as Jehovah God. From a study of similar features in duplicate stories, students of the Old Testament have identified several sources of the Pentateuch and made invaluable contributions to our understanding of this literature.

A contribution of similar value has been made by a study of the literary sources of the first three gospels. The authors of these gospels wrote much as the authors of Hebrew history wrote. They copied their sources with little re-writing, often in alternate blocks. One of the common sources used by Matthew and Luke was Mark; another was a document (since lost) which probably antedated Mark. The identification of these sources made a sane interpretation of Gospel parallelisms possible and dealt a deathblow to superficial harmonizing of the Gospels.

The nature of these parallels can be seen in the following examples:

MATT. 9:14-17	MARK 2:18-22	LUKE 5:33-39
Then come to him the disciples of John,	And John's disciples and the Pharisees were fasting: and they come and say unto him, Why do John's disciples and the disciples of the Pharisees fast,	And they said unto him, The disciples of John
saying, Why do we and the Pharisees fast oft,		fast often, and make supplications; likewise also the *disciples* of the Pharisees but thine eat and drink.
but thy disciples fast not? And Jesus said unto them, Can the sons of the bridechamber mourn, as long as the bridegroom is with them?	but thy disciples fast not? And Jesus said unto them, Can the sons of the bridechamber fast, while the bridegroom is with them? as long as they have the bridegroom with them, they cannot fast.	And Jesus said unto them, Can ye make the sons of the bridechamber fast, while the bridegroom is with them?
but the days will come, when the bridegroom shall be taken away from them, and then will they fast.	But the days will come, when the bridegroom shall be taken away from them, and then will they fast	But the days will come; and when the bridegroom shall be taken away from them, then will they fast

MATT. 9:14–17	MARK 2:18–22	LUKE 5:33–39
	in that day.	in those days. And he spake also a parable unto them:
And no man putteth a piece of undressed cloth	No man seweth a piece of undressed cloth	No man rendeth a piece from a new garment and putteth it
upon an old garment; for that which should fill it up taketh from the garment,	on an old garment: else that which should fill it up taketh from it, the new from the old,	upon an old garment; else he will rend the new,
and a worse rent is made.	and a worse rent is made.	and also the piece from the new will not agree with the old.
Neither do *men* put new wine into old wine-skins: else the skins burst, and the wine is spilled, and the skins perish: but they put new wine into fresh wine-skins, and both are preserved.	And no man putteth new wine into old wine-skins; else the wine will burst the skins, and the wine perisheth, and the skins: but *they put* new wine into fresh wine-skins.	And no man putteth new wine into old wine-skins; else the new wine will burst the skins, and itself will be spilled, and the skins will perish. But new wine must be put into fresh wine-skins.
		And no man having drunk old *wine* desireth new; for he saith, The old is good.

The comparison of the parallels between the Gospels led also to the discovery that Matthew and Luke relied upon some common source other than Mark. The nature of their agreement against Mark can be seen in their report of the preaching of John the Baptist. In Mark this is briefly summarized as the preaching of a baptism of repentance unto remission of sins; in Matthew and Luke the content of an exhortation is given.

MATT. 3:7–10	LUKE 3:7–9
But when he saw many of the Pharisees and Sadducees, coming to his baptism, he said unto them,	He said therefore to the multitudes that went out to be baptised of him
Ye offspring of vipers, who warned you to flee from the wrath to come? 8 Bring forth therefore fruit worthy of repentance: 9 and think not to say within yourselves, We have Abraham to our father: for I say unto you, that God is able of these stones to raise up children unto Abraham. 10 And even now the axe lieth at the root of the trees: every tree therefore that bringeth not forth good fruit is hewn down, and cast into the fire.	Ye offspring of vipers, who warned you to flee from the wrath to come? 8 Bring forth therefore fruits worthy of repentance, and begin not to say within yourselves, We have Abraham to our father: for I say unto you, that God is able of these stones to raise up children unto Abraham. 9 And even now the axe also lieth at the root of the trees: every tree therefore that bringeth not forth good fruit is hewn down, and cast into the fire.

From the most minute study of evidence of this sort, invaluable results for the literary criticism of the New Testament have been obtained. It is, indeed, no exaggeration to say that the major achievements made in the early generations of scholarly study of the Bible and the history of Judaism and Christianity were attained by the use of such literary criticism as that which we have briefly discussed and illustrated here. But the significance of this source analysis has sometimes been overemphasized or misinterpreted. Superficial features of the data are seized upon as possessing basic significance. The illustrations given above show that some passages occur in all three of the Synoptic Gospels—Matthew, Mark, and Luke. This triplication of the story has been called "the triple tradition"; and, since a threefold cord is stronger than one with a single strand, it has been assumed that what was in the triple tradition was historically more reliable than that which appeared in but one of these Gospels. This would be true if the authors had access to accurate sources of information and were concerned primarily with attaining factual accuracy. But their purposes were religious rather than historical, and the quality of their sources undoubtedly varied. It is quite possible that an event related in a single Gospel, any one of the four, might surpass in the accuracy of its detail any story that appeared in three or even all four of the Gospels.

Another example of the perversion of source analysis can be found in the tendency to favor the "oldest" source. From the assumption that the earliest must be the most accurate, Mark's Gospel has been given an extravagant recognition ever since its priority in date was demonstrated by scholarship.

When one of the theories of Gospel origins labeled the non-Markan source common to Matthew and Luke with the name "Q" and claimed that it was probably earlier than Mark, many transferred to it the extravagant loyalty earlier rendered to Mark. But our earliest literary sources leave us all too far from the period of the events described, and the nature of their contents is such as to call for the most rigorous scrutiny. It is worth the student's notice that in modern courts the testimony of even the most reputable eyewitness is accepted only when it has withstood the most searching examination and has been checked against all available controls. No careless acceptance of all the contents of any particular document or source as the "oldest" source will be possible for the serious student.

This is still more evident when the goal of the student of Scripture is the understanding of all primitive Christian experience—not that of Jesus alone—or the comprehension of all phases of Hebrew religion—not that of any "pure" period alone. This more inclusive goal has become the commonly accepted aim of biblical students in our generation. When the purposes of Bible study are so defined, any special source, or particular element in the tradition, loses pre-eminence; all sources are a priori equally valuable. To the student of the Scriptures in this generation, the literary criticism of the Bible presents a set of sharpened tools which he should use in the attempt to create a full and accurate account of Christian life and Hebrew religion in Bible days. The methods and materials employed in this broad and ultimate task are the subject of the next chapter.

BIBLIOGRAPHY ON LITERARY CRITICISM

GENERAL

GOODSPEED, E. J. *The Story of the Bible*. Chicago: University of Chicago Press, 1936.

Brief but clear statement of positions generally held by scholars on the questions of literary introduction: date, author, place, etc.

————. *Introduction to the New Testament*. Chicago: University of Chicago Press, 1937.

More advanced than the *Story*.

————. *A History of Early Christian Literature*. Chicago: University of Chicago Press, 1942.

BEWER, J. A. *The Literature of the Old Testament in Its Historical Development* (rev. ed.). New York: Columbia University Press, 1933.

A rather detailed presentation in chronological order, with copious quotations.

SCOTT, E. F. *The Literature of the New Testament*. New York: Columbia University Press, 1932.

Similar to the work of Goodspeed but a little more detailed in treatment.

BRIGHTMAN, E. S. *Sources of the Hexateuch*. New York, Cincinnati, etc.: Abingdon Press, 1918.

BURTON, E. D., AND GOODSPEED, E. J. *Harmony of the Synoptic Gospels*. New York: Scribners, 1917.

This book, with the preceding one, will make easily available to the student the evidence on which the study of the sources of the Pentateuch and the first three gospels rests.

JAMES, M. R. *The Aprocryphal New Testament*. Oxford: University Press, 1924.

Brief introductions with English translations of a large number of books more or less marginally connected with the New Testament.

————. *The Lost Apocrypha of the Old Testament, Their Titles and Fragments, Collected, Translated, and Discussed*. New York: Macmillan, 1920.

KRÜGER, G. *History of Early Christian Literature in the First Three Centuries* (trans. by C. R. GILLETT). New York: Macmillan, 1897.

OESTERLEY, W. O. E. *An Introduction to the Books of the Apocrypha*. New York: Macmillan, 1935.

A thorough literary introduction to the books of the Old Testament which are accepted as authoritative Scripture in the Catholic but not in the Protestant Church.

OTTLEY, R. R. *A Handbook to the Septuagint*. London: Methuen & Co., 1920.

An introduction to the study of the Greek version of the Old Testament.

STRACK, H. L. *Introduction to Talmud and Midrasch*. Philadelphia: Jewish Publication Society, 1931.

Authorized translation from the author's revision of the fifth German edition.

ADVANCED

OESTERLEY, W. O. E., AND ROBINSON, T. H. *An Introduction to the Books of the Old Testament*. London: S.P.C.K.; New York: Macmillan, 1934.

A fresh and thorough critical manual.

MOFFATT, J. *Introduction to the Literature of the New Testament*. New York: Scribners, 1918.

A fine piece of work, still the standard, though now in sad need of revision.

GRANT, F. C. *The Growth of the Gospels*. New York, Cincinnati, etc.: Abingdon Press, 1933.

A fine introduction to technical study of the Gospels; good Bibliography.

CHARLES, R. H., *et al.* *The Apocrypha and Pseudepigrapha of the Old Testament in English with Introductions and Critical and Explanatory Notes to the Several Books*, Vol. I: *Apocrypha;* Vol. II: *Pseudepigrapha*. Oxford: Clarendon Press, 1913.

BARDENHEWER, O. *Geschichte der altkirchlichen Literatur*. Freiburg im Breisgau: Herder, 1902–32. Vol. I (2d ed.), 1913;

Vol. II (2d ed.), 1914; Vol. III (2d ed.), 1923; Vol. IV, 1924; Vol. V, 1932.

The most up to date of exhaustive histories of early Christian literature.

EPSTEIN, I. (ed.). *The Talmud.* London: Soncino Press, 1935——.

This English translation, edited with introductions and notes, is to be completed in about thirty volumes. First set of 8 vols. (*Nezikin*) published in 1935; second set (*Nashim*) published in 1936.

CADBURY, H. J. *The Style and Literary Method of Luke.* ("Harvard Theological Studies," Vol. VI.) Cambridge: Harvard University Press, 1920.

A brilliant piece of literary and linguistic criticism which annihilated the "medical language" of Luke.

RIDDLE, D. W. *The Gospels, Their Origin and Growth.* Chicago: University of Chicago Press, 1939.

Gives special attention to the results of form criticism.

FILSON, F. V. *The Origin of the Gospels.* New York: Abingdon Press, 1938.

A general survey of recent study of the gospels.

Chapter VI

The Interpretation of the Bible
The Historical Method
Historical Criticism

☼

THE historian of pagan antiquity limits himself to no narrow field. He is vitally concerned with political history. He studies governments and international relations; the reigns of kings and emperors attract his attention. But he no longer focuses attention upon this one aspect of life to the exclusion of others. Other more prosaic areas make their contribution to his reconstruction of the past. Geography, for example, is studied in its broadest terms; cities, rivers, climates, crops, roads, etc., all come within the scope of his investigation.

The two aspects of life that have been touched on here (political and geographical) do not exhaust the territory that the historian attempts to cover but suggest the diversity of the elements that attract his attention. These elements have not all exercised the same degree of fascination for each historian, or even for each generation of historians. Some scholars have emphasized political phenomena as the dominant factor in the story of the past; others have focused the reader's attention on economic factors as the primary ones. At the present time an increasing amount of attention is given to social history. The record of the past is no longer presented as incarnate in the biographies of a few distinguished leaders; it is found to the same degree in the story of the masses.

This type of history is primarily interested in group life and group movements. It sees political, economic, and religious history as social process. Institutions as it portrays them are not static and stolid but move through a constant change, as new generations, faced with new problems, adapt them to their needs. The ultimate interest of the social historian is to revitalize the past by recapturing the living experiences of the individual in relation to the various groups to which he belonged. He sees literature as a deposit made by the rich life of the time in which it was produced; he studies it not as an end but as a means. He strives to comprehend it so that he may comprehend the life that produced it.

This emphasis has driven the historian to the byways as well as to the highways; it has put a new premium on the nonliterary sources for ancient history. It is clear, for example, that a scholar who is trying to write the economic history of the Roman Empire will find valuable information in the excavation of a store that dealt in agricultural implements as well as in the sonorous description of the charms of rural life by one of the gilded youths of Rome. The recovery of tens of thousands of tax receipts from ancient Egypt on pieces of papyrus and ostraca has made possible the writing of the story of taxation even for separate sections and cities. Sources of this type are made available to the historian by the archeologist, and the study of archeology has become more and more important as the study of the social and economic life of antiquity has gained in emphasis. The result is that from numerous expeditions a rich stream of archeological finds has been poured at the historians' feet.

THE SCOPE OF BIBLICAL HISTORY

Historical criticism of the Scriptures is as extensive in scope and diversified in interests as the history of any secular movement. The emphasis on political history which characterized many of the school texts of my childhood has been equally widespread on the pages of sacred history. Most of my devout readers have struggled with lists of the kings of Israel and Judah, or with outlines of evidence for identifying Merneptah or Ramses II as the pharaoh of the Oppression.

Nor was this study made in vain. The current emphasis upon other elements in the social complex should not blind us to the real significance of the so-called "political history" of the Bible. It has crowded meaning into the terms "pre-Exilic," "Exilic," and "post-Exilic," and against these backgrounds many an Old Testament book has become more intelligible. The story of the Maccabean rebellion adds meaning to the pages of every Jewish and Christian apocalypse. A knowledge of Roman administration in Palestine under Herod and his sons and successors clarifies much of the gospel story.

Secular interest in geography has been matched in the biblical field. Every detailed modern introduction to the Bible has included a discussion of the geography of Palestine, and historical geographies of the Holy Land have filled imposing volumes. If biblical scholars have erred in this area, it is in giving too much attention to miscellaneous geographical data.

These interests in political and geographical history can be matched in a half-dozen other areas. The economic background of the gospels has been made the subject of special study. The perennial interest in the great personalities of the religion still continues to produce biographies of Jesus, Paul, and David. The magnitude of the contribution made by the individual religious genius is given due recognition, but the major emphases of contemporary study fall in the area of social-historical method.

PRESENT-DAY EMPHASES IN HISTORICAL CRITICISM OF THE BIBLE

The development of a widespread interest in social movements and group processes has been noted above with reference to the writing of secular history. This development has had important results for the study of the Bible; its influence upon the study of Judaism, Christianity, and the Bible has been of epoch-making importance in more than one area.

a) RELIGIONS ARE DEVELOPMENTAL

In the first place, the religions themselves are now studied as movements of a vitally developmental character. The older conception of them as static, divine inserts into history has been repudiated. Emphasis is no longer put upon the originality of the message of Jesus and the prophets; modern historical study of the environment of both the Jewish and the Christian religions has patiently accumulated parallel after parallel, antecedent before antecedent, until the word "unique" as applied to the elements of these cults has lost much of its significance. These religions are now seen as the product of social forces directed by individual genius. The historians have shown how extensively they inherit, borrow, adopt, and adapt.

It is now recognized that Judaism and Christianity change naturally, inevitably, and constantly. The old idealization of some one period or the literature of one period as representing the "pure" religion has been seriously modified if not rejected. With it has vanished its corollary, the disparagement of all changes subsequent to the period of "purity" as corruptions, dilutions, perversions, etc., and therefore essentially bad. The religion is seen to change as the believers' vital religious experience is conditioned by new social situations. Christianity is defined not as a creed, or as the religion of any one individual, group, or period, but as the vital religious life of the successive generations of Christians.

b) LIFE PRECEDES LITERATURE

A second result of social historical study is the general recognition of the priority of the religion to the religious literature. It has been one of the shortcomings of Protestantism so to stress the importance and authority of the Bible that many devout Christians have come to believe that Christianity originated in and from the New Testament. The most superficial study, however, will show that Christianity existed for at least a century without a New Testament as a sacred book. Christianity had left Palestine and spread far and wide in the Roman world before the first book of the New Testament was even written, much less published or accepted as authoritative. Strong Christian communities dotted the shores of the Mediterranean before the Four Gospels were written.

Thus the period of Christian history to which the Protestant has most often pointed as representing "pure" Christianity—the first century of the cult's existence—is a period in which there was no New Testament. This indicates a very different evaluation of the role of the New Testament in Christianity on the part of the primitive Christian and the conventional modern Protestant. Exactly the same facts exist in regard to the Old Testament. The important period of Jewish life suggested by the words "exodus," "conquest," and "kingdom" knew no sacred literature. Moses, Abraham, Elijah, and David lived their religion without the sacred book.

c) EXPERIENCE CREATES LITERATURE

In ever widening circles the creative role of the religious experience of the group and individual in regard to the literature is frankly admitted. The significant part played in the production of the literature by social experience is admitted by more scholars today than was the case a generation ago, and the creative function of the religious group is seen at work throughout more and more of the canonical literature.

From the moment that the historical method of interpretation was applied to the letters of Paul, it was obvious that the problem situations in the churches founded by Paul had almost as much to do with the contents of Paul's letters as Paul himself did. This is seen clearly in Galatians, a letter which focuses all the fiery enthusiasm of Paul's religion on a single issue as sharply as a glass brings the sun's rays to a single burning point. It can be seen with equal clarity in the complexity of I Corinthians, where the first part of the letter is taken up with Paul's attempts to straighten out troublesome situations at Corinth that have been reported to him (factions, lawsuits, immorality), and the second part is concerned with the apostle's answers to half-a-dozen specific questions asked him in a letter from the church at Corinth. In these letters by Paul we can clearly see the Christian trying to work out a pattern of living in a society already crowded with religions. The thorough integration of these pagan cults in the social life of the time caused many of the problems of the Pauline converts.

Butchering had religious implications, political life was religious—both locally and imperially—recreation was religious, etc. The everyday experiences of devout Christians in this religious fulness of the time determined the table of contents of most of the letters written by Paul. This does not deny the significant contribution made to those letters by the rich religious experience of the apostle himself, yet it must be remembered that that experience was itself in some part social.

This has long been recognized by interpreters of the Pauline writings. The situation at Corinth, in Galatia, etc., is now studied along with or before the message written by the apostle. The creative influence of the social environment has been recognized also in the later books of the New Testament and in the Old Testament writings that represent late Judaism. Among Protestant interpreters, it has often been popular to interpret these books as the product of periods of corruption of the pure religion of earlier days. Thus it is claimed that the true vision of God won by the prophets was obscured by the priests and scribes who came after them; that the pure word of God uttered by Jesus was diluted by the incipient Catholicism of the late first and early second centuries. These changes were explained as due to compromise with environment, assimilation of external influences, etc. Hence, in these areas, the recognition of the significant influence of environment upon the creation of the sacred literature was easy for the champions of such views.

But the recognition of the similar situation in the Gospels and the Prophets came more slowly. The historical study of literary problems helped to make this possible. The removal of the Fourth Gospel from a close association with the others to the very end of the first century or the beginning of the second hastened a sane evaluation of the part played by the religious experience of post-resurrection Christianity in the composition of that gospel. The study of the literary sources of the first three gospels led to the identification of "secondary" elements in the gospel tradition, and it was freely admitted that the changing experiences and beliefs of second-generation Christianity had affected the formation of these strands of the tradition. But in some areas a certain insulation of the revealed message is claimed for the earliest layer of the gospel content; this, it is felt, came straight and undiluted from the mind of God.

This position has been abandoned by the majority of scholars for two reasons. The first is that the increased knowledge of Judaism has made it plain that Jesus—like the prophets before him—was himself influenced by the social situation in which he formulated his message. The second is that the increased knowledge of the Christianity of the second generation and of its gentile environment has made it plain that the part played by the church in the creation of the gospels was a major part. Today no one can stop with Mark or "Q" and say "here is the pure gospel."

The Gospels were produced to meet the needs of Christians removed by at least one full generation from the death of Jesus. But the gap is deeper than it is wide, for the gospels were produced to meet the needs of self-conscious, gentile churches, struggling for their existence in the strenuous religious competition of the cities of the Graeco-Roman world. The infant cult needed organization, sanctions for cult practices, information, definition of the distinctively Christian way of life, defense from state and rivals, solution of the problem of its relation to Judaism, etc. Most of these problems were unknown to Jesus and his followers, or were seen by them in different degrees of intensity and under different aspects.

Most of all, the church needed an adequate definition of Jesus in terms of its own contemporary faith and experience. By the time that Paul's letters were written, Jesus is already defined as a divine Lord and Savior as well as the Messiah of Old Testament hopes. Yet Paul can find no validation for his faith in the story of Jesus' life that has reached him. For him the proof of Jesus' lordship lies in his own experience of communion with Jesus and salvation through union with him. The resurrection was the demonstration of Jesus' divinity; before the resurrection there was nothing but a humble career.

The evangelists modify this definition. In Mark the humility of Jesus' earthly career is lightened by previews of the resurrection. As in Paul, Jesus is not really the Messiah until the resurrection, but occasionally there is a partial revelation of his divine nature. The demons recognize him; their own supernatural nature allows them to identify him. On the mountain top he appears for a moment to the inner circle of his followers as he really is. Yet throughout the major part of Mark, the messiahship of Jesus is a secret, a dark mystery even to his most intimate associates. This frame of definition is part of the evangelist's contribution to the Gospel story.

The distinctive nature of the Markan definition of Jesus can be seen by contrasting it not only with that of Paul but also with that of John. In the Fourth Gospel the Lord of the Christian cult is openly the Messiah, the divine world-savior, from the first scene of the Gospel to the last. He himself teaches this without hesitation and with monotonous repetition. His disciples and his hearers generally (except the Jews) have no difficulty in recognizing him as the divine son of God, the Messiah, the Light of the World, etc. This frame of definition is part of this evangelist's contribution to the Gospel story.

Later in the second century some unknown Christians wrote gospels which told the story of Jesus' infancy. These carry the definition of Jesus as being openly a god on earth several steps farther than John had done. In these infancy gospels Jesus knows he is a god when he is a little boy. Moreover, he shows his deity in numerous actions and teachings. His birds made of mud come to life; anyone who injures him in play is slain with a word; teachers are baffled again and again by his wisdom. The boy Jesus is a god in that he possesses supernatural power and supernatural wisdom. This frame of definition is part of these evangelists' contribution to the Gospel story.

d) GROUP INFLUENCE BEFORE THE GOSPELS

In the last generation the attention of scholars has been drawn to the study of the Gospel story as it existed in the days before the Gospels were written. It is now generally admitted that in its earliest form the story existed in separate bits of information about Jesus' actions or teachings. Sayings were repeated and cherished in a group of Galileans who had followed Jesus, as disciples long before had followed the prophets. Stories of actions performed by Jesus were repeated by other Christians to show what Jesus meant to them. At various times and places and in various ways, these fragments of tradition were grouped, edited, expanded, abbreviated. The interest of the Christians in these items was basically religious rather than historical; therefore, it was easy for unhistorical elements to enter stories with a basis of fact; it was possible for stories to be generally accepted which had no basis in the facts of Jesus' life; it was easy for accurate stories of what Jesus had said and done to die for lack of repetition when these accurate stories served no need of the group to which they came.

One of the first and clearest implications of the existence of the Gospel stories in little independent sections (called "pericopes") is that we owe the time and place sequences in our gospels to the relatively late and unreliable work of the evangelists. Many of these little stories in the gospels are still without any indication of time or place; that many more of them were originally without such indications is a probable assumption. The more frequently a story is repeated, the more specific it becomes. Locations are supplied, anonymous characters are identified, and the time is given. The "framework" of the gospel message is almost entirely the creation of second-generation Christianity.

The immature church's needs were legion. It needed sanctions for its simple ritual. The story of Jesus' last meal with his followers becomes the story of the institution by Jesus of a ceremony for his followers to observe: at first a memorial service, later a sacramental communion. Jesus sets his own teaching above the Jewish law. Jesus' authority is invoked to prevent Christians from going to law in non-Christian courts; the story is told with explicit reference to the existence of Christian church groups.

In Palestine in Jesus' day, his followers were not troubled by table etiquette. The question of obeying or not obeying the Old Testament dietary laws was not a pressing one to them. The Palestinian customs were well established and included prescriptions as to the nature and extent of table fellowship between Jews and Gentiles. But, when Christianity moved outside both Palestine and Judaism and welcomed masses of Gentiles into its communion, questions as to the validity of the Jewish dietary legislation arose frequently and clamored for an answer. We hear the clamor echoing through Paul's letters. Paul's own claim that these laws were invalid for Gentile Christians ultimately became the position of the church. But the church was not satisfied with a Pauline authorization of the repudiation of these laws and found in a pronouncement of Jesus himself that revocation of the Old Testament legislation for which it yearned.

The saying appears in Mark 7:14–15 and is explained in 7:17–23 (cf. Matt. 15:10–20). Jesus calls the crowd to him and says, "It is not anything from outside of a man entering into him which can defile him, but the things which come forth from the man are the things which defile the man." After his withdrawal into the house, he explains the saying to the disciples, pointing out that food for the body does not touch the soul, but that vices like envy, adultery, etc., which spring from within, are the real defilement. In the original form of the saying there was here no more than a strong declaration of the superiority of spiritual values to mere ritual conformity.

But as Mark tells the story, and he may be accurately reporting the form in which it reached him, this is an emancipation of Jesus' followers from all food laws. The specific authorization is made by a brief explanatory note in 7:19, "making clean all foods." This clause directly applies Jesus' pronouncement to the later Christian controversy over clean and unclean foods. It is interesting to note that Matthew does not follow Mark in this particular application. He omits the explanatory clause, and, by the addition of one brief sentence at the end of the explanation to the disciples, he refers the whole discussion to ritual washings. Thus the same saying of Jesus emancipates Christians from Jewish food laws (in Mark) and from Jewish ritual washings (in Matthew).

The last generation has seen the careful study of

the content of the first three gospels, section by section, in the attempt to establish the extent of the church's contribution to the picture of Jesus. In Germany it has been carried on by the champions of a discipline called *Formgeschichte* ("form criticism" or "form history"), which gets its name from the least important aspect of its work. It has tried to classify the forms in which the separate units of the tradition exist; hence its name. But its contribution in the study of forms has been of minor importance. Much more significant has been its insistence upon the important role of group needs and interests in the formation of Gospel stories. This is not a new discovery of the *Formgeschichte* school; they share this method and emphasis with the "social historian" and with many a scholar who is still content with the simple title "historian."

If today the Gospels are approached solely as a source of information about the historical Jesus, the result will be meager in quantity and definitely unsatisfactory in quality to the pious layman. He may find some consolation in the fact that no historian will identify this residue as the total picture of Jesus' personality or career. The church's creative role included rejection. Whatever Jesus was, he was certainly more than the fragments which the historian accepts after his rigorous inspection of the tradition.

e) NOTHING IS SPURIOUS FOR THE HISTORIAN

But the social historian is, in a sense, more rigorous than the general public has yet realized. His interest and curiosity are catholic in scope. He does not approach the Gospels for the sole purpose of finding out what is historical in the stories about Jesus. His purpose is also to find out what can be known about the vital experiences of Jesus' followers. He rejects none of the Gospel material; the section which tells him nothing about Jesus may be of great value as a source of information on the faith and experience of the mass of unknown Christians in the second generation of Christianity's history.

The student of the Old Testament, for example, in generations past often labeled certain sections of the books as "spurious" and then proceeded to ignore them. This happened all too frequently in the study of the prophets. If Amos 9:8*b*–15 was a later addition to the great prophecy, then the student of Amos ignored it. Unfortunately, no other student picked it up, and no attention at all was given to these "spurious" passages. But today their authenticity as representatives of the age in which they were produced is emphasized, and they are carefully studied for what they can tell us of these later periods.

Partly as a reaction to the tendency of past generations to center attention on the isolated individuals who attained prominence and immortality for their names in the leadership of the cult, the modern historian focuses attention on the anonymous masses, on social movements, on group needs, on the common faith, on the laymen whose contribution to the cult was as significant as that of the leaders. The knowledge of the New Testament is not, therefore, the goal of his study. Once that knowledge is gained, it becomes a tool, a source, to be used in writing the history of the vital religious movements of early Christian history.

f) IMPORTANCE OF ARCHEOLOGY

The student of Christianity or Judaism who accepts the emphases of social history turns more and more to the use of the nonliterary sources. He cannot study the movements and experiences of cult groups in a vacuum. The society in which they existed becomes of vital importance to him. He prizes the results attained by the student of the social and economic history of the ancient East and the Graeco-Roman world.

These historians have shown the tremendous value of archeological sources for the reconstruction of social life in all its phases. The student who investigates religious societies has turned his own attention in increasing measure to the study of nonliterary sources of information on the religions in which he is interested. But in the study of early Christian history the Protestant historian has used this material last and least.

Part of this tardiness has been due to a narrow sectarian loyalty. Roman Catholic learning had long ago appealed to archeological evidence in support of its doctrines and claims. For example, inscriptions from the Eternal City were used to support the claim that Peter was the founder of the Roman papacy. Other nonliterary sources established an earlier exist-

ence of liturgy and officialdom than fervent Protestants of an extreme type were willing to accept. In the
bitterness of the debate they attacked not only the
interpretation of archeological evidence but also the
entire discipline—in so far as it applied to Christian
origins.

In the more innocuous field of Old Testament history, however, archeological techniques were not only
employed but even employed in the very manner in
which earlier Roman Catholic scholars had used them
in their study of early Christian history. Book after
book on "Archeology and the Bible" took as its
thesis the defensive assertion that the results of
archeological study confirmed or supported the Bible
(almost always giving 90 per cent of the space to the
Old Testament) in its statements as to dates, kings'
reigns, geography, etc. This use of archeology was
atomistic. Any isolated item that was related to any
Old Testament passage was featured as another valuable confirmation of the Bible.

The use of archeology which is today making a
valuable contribution to the interpretation of the
Bible has a very different basis. Its purposes and
methods are far removed from those defined in the
preceding paragraph. Illumination—not confirmation—is its goal. It rejoices not in isolated discoveries, no matter how dramatic, but in the patient
accumulation of a mass of detailed evidence that will
help the historian to reconstruct a vanished culture.
To the interpreter of the Bible it is an auxiliary discipline which supplies him with invaluable source ma-

terial. Archeological evidence on dates is of relatively little importance when compared with the light
shed by this discipline on the life of the world in
which Judaism and Christianity lived, moved, and
had their being.

If we take for granted that the student of the Bible
is interested in archeological evidence as to business
conditions, etc., in the environment of the cult he
studies, we can pass on to a more focal point—the
light that archeology has shed (and is shedding) on
the cults which were predecessors and/or competitors
of Judaism and Christianity.

For the student of the Old Testament this light
has been steadily growing in illuminating power.
There is no need or space here to detail its progress,
but the nature of the recent discoveries at Ras
Shamra may be summarized as an example of the
type of contribution made. Beginning in 1929, exca-
vators working on a little promontory twenty miles
south of the mouth of the Orontes River found a large
number of tablets inscribed in a "cuneiform alpha-
bet." They contain cult prescriptions, liturgy, and
legends of about the thirteenth century B.C. They
supply the student of Semitic languages with a wealth
of evidence, hitherto unknown, as to Syro-Phoeni-
cian usage at this period. The study of the Ras
Shamra myth and cult patterns has already illumi-
nated many a dark spot in the Old Testament literature and has raised anew in challenging fashion the
question as to an important genetic relationship between the religion of the Old Testament and the

indigenous Canaanite culture. One of the ritual commands of the Ras Shamra tablets is "Boil a kid in the milk"; this is one item in the magical technique for producing early rains. The Old Testament proscriptions of boiling a kid in its mother's milk (Exod. 23:19; 34:26; Deut. 14:21) can no longer be explained as nomadic and therefore presumably Mosaic. It now seems more probable that seething a kid in its mother's milk was part of the cult technique of the early Hebrews, carrying a function analogous to that which it served at Ras Shamra. The attack on the practice in the Old Testament passages referred to above would be a later modification of a primitive cult practice. Not only in matters of ritual detail but in the broader areas of world-view, of dualism, of hope of life as a religious gift, of messianism, etc., these fruits of the archeologist's patient labor are making important and often startling contributions to our knowledge.

From Graeco-Roman archeology has come an analogous illumination of the field of early Christian history. In this area, also, our knowledge of the competing cults has been greatly increased by the study of archeological sources. This has been noteworthy in the study of those personal salvation cults, the mystery religions, which were so popular in the Graeco-Roman world in the time of the Roman Empire. They present the historian with dismayingly scanty literary remains; the emphasis upon secrecy and "mystery" in the cult discouraged the writing of adequate descriptions by the initiates. For the most part their testimony consists of obscure passwords and mottoes which demand rather than supply illumination.

But the archeologist has made up for the meager amount of literary remains, as can be seen, for example, in the case of the cult of Mithras. The volumes in which Franz Cumont has edited the archeological evidence for the worship of the Persian god present the student with a wealth of information. The location of Mithras monuments on a map dots its surface from the Euxine Sea to the mountains of Scotland, and from the banks of the Rhine to the Sahara Desert. Thus the extent of the distribution of the cult is indicated with an accuracy impossible for one who used literary sources alone. The fact that these sources can be dated, at least approximately, adds to their value. Moreover, they give indirect suggestions concerning the cult ritual—suggestions which are made the more valuable by the prejudiced nature of the literary references to cult practices. Most of the latter come from Christians engaged in the most bitter competition with the sun-god's cult. With the help of the archeological witnesses, Mr. Willoughby, in his study of regeneration in the pagan world, has given a vivid reconstruction of one of the cave chapels in which the worshipers of Mithras met and presents the rites and beliefs of the cult in an impressive manner.

The newcomer in the field of early Christian archeology is constantly stimulated by unexpected elements in the nonliterary tradition. As he leafs through the facsimiles of catacomb paintings, he is astonished to find Jonah and the hippocampus leading all other characters in popularity. Pagan cupids and Orpheus "good shepherds" have an important message to give as to the nature and extent of pagan influence. There is significance in the absence of any crucifixion scene in the early period, as also in the extreme rarity of crosses. That Jesus used a magician's wand like Circe's is somewhat surprising. Rather unexpected to the novice is the amount and early date of Christian paintings and the presence of frescoes and mosaics in Jewish synagogues.

Nor do the inscriptions fall behind the pictures in the value of the information they impart. On the basis of a study of a collection of Jewish inscriptions, E. R. Goodenough has made several tentative but most stimulating suggestions; e.g., that "normative" Judaism was unknown until after the publication of the Talmud and that Judaism at the time of the formation of the New Testament was borrowing heavily from Hellenism.

Christian inscriptions likewise are a valuable source of information on the life and customs of the early Christians. Dean Case, in writing the story of the place of Christianity in the business life of the ancient world, found in the inscriptions alone adequate information as to the occupations of the early Christians.

The French archeologist Le Blant and, after him, Sir William Ramsay found in certain types of names in the Christian inscriptions valuable evidence as to pagan attitudes toward Christianity. The terms of contempt which the pagans applied to the Christians were often accepted by the latter and worn as names. Among these "epithet names" are the following: "gullible," "unreasonable," "criminal," "trickster," "insolent," "churlish," "pernicious," "filth," "evil," "knavish," "brute," "contemptible," "deserter," "refuse," and "dirty." By accepting these names (according to Le Blant's theory) the individual Christians made a boast out of slander. Leclerq has more recently quarreled with Le Blant's theory and favors the explanation that these names were charms. They would save the bearer from the envy and abuse of the minor supernatural powers; the demons would be misled by these unattractive names and so would tolerate these unfortunates and abstain from attacking them. Whichever explanation finally wins the support of scholarship, the data themselves are evidence of no slight value.

Harnack found in the study of Christian names valuable evidence as to the attitude of the Christians toward the pagans. He has shown that the use of Christian names taken from the Bible does not go back to the first centuries. Until after the middle of the third century, Christians made an almost exclusive use of the old pagan names. Among the names of Christians appearing in inscriptions are the names of pagan deities; e.g., Heraclius, Mercurius, Aphrodisius, Dionysius. "The martyrs perished because they refused to sacrifice to the gods whose names they bore." This paradox can be explained only by admitting that the general custom of the world in which the Christians were living proved stronger than any reflections of their own. The sense of real inner distinction as a Christian was so strong that it made the name relatively unimportant. But from A.D. 250 on, as the church conforms more and more to the world, the use of distinctively Christian names became first preferable and then normative. More than one force led to this reversal. The changing of names was a common pagan practice, especially after A.D. 212; the growing importance of infant baptism favored the use of Christian names; and, as the world moved into the church, it carried with it a superstitious evaluation of the power of names. Thus a second paradox confronts the first. As the individual Christian came to resemble his pagan neighbor more and more closely, his name proclaimed his Christianity most emphatically. Whereas, in the period when the individual Christian was set off against the pattern of the surrounding demonic culture, his name proclaimed a loyalty to these demonic powers.

Archeological evidence as to the use of Bible names by Christians clearly reflects also the anti-Jewish sentiment of the church. This is more evident in the West than in the East, but it is New Testament—not Old Testament—names that are first used —Peter and Paul, for example—and Old Testament names run a bad third to names of local Christian heroes and saints. If Shakespeare had asked the Christian archeologist "What's in a name?" the answer would have been "Plenty!"

From archeology's cornucopia a wealth of evidence is poured out before the student of the Bible. Today he includes it with the fruit of other disciplines (literary and historical) as resource material to be used in his attempt to master not the literature of the canon alone, not the literature of the cult alone, but the whole of the religious life whose richness and vigor produced the books and gives them meaning.

BIBLIOGRAPHY ON HISTORICAL CRITICISM

GENERAL

BARTON, G. A. *Archaeology and the Bible* (6th ed.). Philadelphia: Sunday School Union, 1933.

Valuable for its extensive quotation of illuminating parallels; more important for Old Testament than for New Testament.

CASE, S. J. *The Social Origins of Christianity*. Chicago: University of Chicago Press, 1923.

Chapter i, "The 'New' New Testament Study," is especially valuable here.

EDMAN, I. *The Mind of Paul*. New York: Holt, 1935.

A very stimulating and readable interpretation of Paul's religion.

GRANT, F. C. (trans.). *Form Criticism: A New Method of New Testament Research* (including "The Study of the Synoptic Gospels," by RUDOLF BULTMANN, and "Primitive Christianity in the Light of Gospel Research," by KARL KUNDSIN). Chicago: Willett, Clark & Co., 1934.

The simplest introduction to this method by its own exponents.

HERFORD, R. TRAVERS. *Judaism in the New Testament Period*. London: Lindsay Press, 1928.

Valuable for its sympathetic appraisal of Pharisaism in the New Testament period.

LIETZMANN, H. *The Beginnings of the Christian Church* (trans. by B. L. WOOLF). New York: Scribner's, 1937.

Clear, vivid, scholarly, and yet concise presentation of Christian history to A.D. 180.

LOWRIE, WALTER. *Monuments of the Early Church*. New York: Macmillan, 1901 (reprinted 1923).

A good general introduction to Christian archeology, illustrated with 182 figures.

MARUCCHI, ORAZIO. *Christian Epigraphy: An Elementary Treatise with a Collection of Ancient Christian Inscriptions Mainly of Roman Origin* (trans. by J. A. WILLIS). Cambridge: At the University Press, 1912.

A brief, general introduction, followed by a classified collection of Roman inscriptions, illustrated with thirty plates.

MATHEWS, SHAILER. *A History of New Testament Times in Palestine* (rev. ed.). New York: Macmillan, 1933.

A concise but thorough study of the political history of the period.

MATTHEWS, I. G. *Old Testament Life and Literature* (2d ed.). New York: Macmillan, 1934.

Life and literature are discussed together in chronological pattern; a useful manual.

RIDDLE, D. W. *Early Christian Life as Reflected in Its Literature*. Chicago: Willett, Clark & Co., 1936.

This volume uses the literature as a source for the study of early Christian life rather than as an end in itself.

PARSONS, E. W. *The Religion of the New Testament*. New York: Harper & Bros., 1939.

An introduction that stresses content.

ADVANCED

CASE, S. J. *The Evolution of Early Christianity*. Chicago: University of Chicago Press, 1914.

Significant definition and interpretation of Christianity as a vitally developmental movement. Valuable bibliographies to 1914.

————. *Jesus: A New Biography*. Chicago: University of Chicago Press, 1927.

An important study, which uses social-historical method. Good bibliography.

————. *The Social Triumph of the Ancient Church*. New York:

CRAIG, CLARENCE T. "Biblical Theology and the Rise of Historicism," *Journal of Biblical Literature*, LXII, No. 4 (December, 1943), 281–94.

DEISSMANN, A. *St. Paul* (new and rev. ed.). London: Hodder & Stoughton, 1926).

Sympathetic interpretation of St. Paul's religion.

DIBELIUS, M. *From Tradition to Gospel* (trans. by B. L. WOOLF). London: I. Nicholson & Watson, 1934.

An exposition of *Formgeschichte* by one of the masters of the method.

DODD, C. H. *The Parables of the Kingdom.* New York: Scribner's, 1936.

Makes use of recent studies and presents valuable interpretation of the parables.

EASTON, B. S. *Christ in the Gospels.* New York: Scribner's, 1930.

Thoroughgoing criticism of *Formgeschichte* and social-historical method, a comprehensive critical survey of recent study of Jesus and the Gospels, written from a conservative viewpoint.

ENSLIN, M. S. *The Ethics of Paul.* New York: Harpers, 1930.

The best of recent studies of Pauline ethics.

FOAKES–JACKSON, F. J., AND LAKE, KIRSOPP (eds.). *The Beginnings of Christianity*, Part I: "The Acts of the Apostles." New York: Macmillan. Vol. I (1920), *Prolegomena I: Jewish, Gentile, and Christian Backgrounds;* Vol. II (1922), *Prolegomena II: Criticism;* Vol. III (1926), *The Text of Acts* (J. H. ROPES); Vol. IV (1933), *English Translation and Commentary* (K. LAKE AND H. J. CADBURY); Vol. V (1933), *Additional Notes to the Commentary* (K. LAKE AND H. J. CADBURY [eds.]).

The special studies in the prolegomena and the additional notes give this work a much broader significance than that of the usual commentary on Acts. Valuable bibliography.

GRAHAM, W. C., AND MAY, H. G. *Culture and Conscience.* Chicago: University of Chicago Press, 1936.

These collaborators have made valuable use of archeological finds in presenting the religion of the Hebrews in relation to its environment.

GRANT, F. C. *The Economic Background of the Gospels.* London: Oxford University Press, 1926.

A brief presentation of economic data in regard to Palestinian life in gospel times.

HOOKE, S. H. (ed.). *Myth and Ritual: Essays on the Myth and Ritual of the Hebrews in Relation to the Culture Pattern of the Ancient East.* By A. M. BLACKMAN AND OTHERS. London: Oxford University Press, 1933.

KLAUSNER, J. *Jesus of Nazareth* (trans. by H. DANBY). New York: Macmillan, 1926.

A scholarly study of Jesus from the Jewish viewpoint.

MOORE, G. F. *Judaism in the First Centuries of the Christian Era.* Cambridge: Harvard University Press, 1927–30.

A comprehensive study of Judaism, advancing the thesis that Judaism is to be defined in terms of the "normative Judaism" of the Pharisees. Full of valuable information and stimulating discussion.

OESTERLEY, W. O. E., AND ROBINSON, T. H. *A History of Israel,* Vol. I: *From the Exodus to the Fall of Jerusalem 586 B.C.,* by Robinson; Vol. II: *From the Fall of Jerusalem 586 B.C. to the Bar-Kokhba Revolt A.D. 135,* by Oesterley. Oxford: Clarendon Press, 1932.

A standard work.

OTTO, RUDOLF. *The Kingdom of God and the Son of Man* (Eng. trans. by B. L. WOOLF and F. V. FILSON). London: Luttenworth Press, 1938.

A stimulating *religious geschichtliche* study, which argues in convincing fashion that Jesus preached a kingdom that had already dawned and thought of himself in terms of the Enochic Son of Man.

WILLOUGHBY, H. R. *Pagan Regeneration.* Chicago: University of Chicago Press, 1929.

A sympathetic and scholarly study of the experience of religious rebirth in the pagan world of New Testament times.

McCOWN, C. C. *The Search for the Real Jesus.* New York: Scribner's, 1940.

A valuable survey of modern study of Jesus.

RIDDLE, D. W. *Paul, Man of Conflict.* Nashville: Cokesbury, 1940.

A sketch of Paul as he reveals himself in his letters.

SMITH, B. T. D. *The Parables of the Synoptic Gospels.* Cambridge (Eng.): University Press, 1937.

Comprehensive and scholarly, yet readable.

Chapter VII

The Interpretation of the Bible
Biblical Theology

✣

A S HAS been stated in the previous chapters, all knowledge of biblical literature in its historical setting is preliminary to an understanding of its meaning today. In the contemporary search for that meaning, historical study in general and social history in particular have declined in use. The preceding chapter noted the importance of the Christian community in the shaping of the New Testament, and most especially the importance of that community's faith in the production of the New Testament. Both these facets appear in the dominant approach to biblical interpretation in the last quarter-century: Biblical Theology. The decline in the use of social history doubtless had many causes. Among them might be mentioned its close association with "liberalism" which has been indicted with superficial optimism and non-theistic philosophy. A second world war and its sequels disposed of social optimism, and in theological faculties a vigorous restatement of Reformation Theology swept the field.

THE BIBLE AS THEOLOGY, NOT HISTORY

The Biblical Theologian reminds us that the Bible is not history in the ordinary, secular meaning of the word. It is not history in the intention of its authors. Their intention was to awaken, or to nurture and strengthen, religious faith. What they wrote was written from the viewpoint of faith to minister to faith.

Thus the biblical authors were in the literal meaning of the term "theologians." Like other believers, they structured their belief. The theology they thus achieved imposed form upon their writing, guided them in selection of material and in the allocation of emphasis.

The presence of four gospels in our Bible gives us a clear example of this fact. Fifty years ago, students of the Bible tended to set the Gospel of John apart from the other three as the theological gospel. At the end of the twentieth chapter, we read, "Now Jesus did many other signs in the presence of the disciples, which are not written in this book; but these are written that you may believe that Jesus is the Christ, the Son of God, and that believing you may have life in his name." Much was made of this frank statement as if it differentiated John from the first three gospels.

The studies of the last generation have emphasized that the same motivation (the same, that is, in being theological) existed for the other evangelists. Mark, once the first choice as the basis for a presentation of the "historical" Jesus is now seen as the champion of a definite and high Christology. In Mark, Jesus is neither Teacher nor Logos, but a Messiah strangely endowed with "authority" and power over demons and disease, temple and Torah, man and nature.

These gospels we have now been told and told emphatically and frequently are not biographies. Moreover their nature is such that the writing of a biography of Jesus would be impossible. The believing community created these books from its faith. What is most clearly reflected in these books is therefore— we are told—the faith of the community. This leads to the oft-quoted dictum that the Gospels are primary sources for the early Christian community in the gospel-writing period, but only secondary sources for the life of Jesus.

With adjustments for the change in circumstances, the same claims are made for the other biblical books.

HISTORIES DO NOT PRODUCE FAITH

The preceding argument is advanced in part to cut the ground from under historicism. This type of interpretation saw historical study as a high road to a purer faith. It has been vigorously attacked as assuming that a knowledge of "facts" about Torah or Prophecy, or most especially, Jesus would determine faith.

But as we have seen above, the biblical "facts" are already mixed with theological interpretation. And still more damning to the claims of historicism, our Christian experience teaches us that the roots of our faith are in the contemporary Christian community —above all in its proclamation of the Word. This ministry which leads us to a confrontation with God here and now is what determines faith and not some historical fact. If our faith depended upon histories, we are reminded, it would be based on an unstable ground which could be shifted by the next discovery of an ancient manuscript. The historian's knowledge is only a knowledge of probability and cannot, therefore, offer certainty to faith.

THEOLOGY IS CENTRAL TO INTERPRETATION

As a result of these emphases, the biblical interpreter sets as his goal understanding the religious ideas and concepts—the theology—of the community that produced the literature he is interpreting. Since he has been himself subject to the same tendentious involvement that he identifies on the part of the biblical authors, it is not strange that he sees very clearly the importance of pure faith in Scripture. A New Reformation theology nourished biblical interpretation as the biblical-theological method gained prominence.

While the identification and exposition of more than one theology (even one for each author) is not forbidden by this methodology, it has tended toward the establishment of a single biblical theology. It has emphasized agreement rather than disagreement; unity rather than diversity. It has often seen the Old Testament from a purely Christian perspective. Theological concern almost always rests upon one

theological structure. Theological interpretation of the
Bible, therefore, tends to find a single coherent set of
concepts or doctrines—even when that set is distinct
from the one with which the interpreter approached
his task. Biblical theology has not shrunk from the
task of expounding THE theology of the Bible. Where
several theologies have been recognized, they have
been few in number and more than one book of the
Bible has come under each one. Thus a Palestinian-
Jewish–Christian theology is contrasted with the
normal Hellenistic Pauline theology, and most of the
New Testament is subsumed under these two headings.

KARL BARTH

Theological interpretation was launched by Karl
Barth. To him more than any other single individual
the creation of a new trend in interpretation is due.
His commentary on Romans was in this sense an
epochal book. Its newness did not lie in the repudiation of previous methods; he admitted the validity of
literary and historical criticism, but he saw its role
as a preparatory one, as preparation for understanding.

Thus Barth attained great influence in interpretation, not through writing about a method of interpretation, but by a more direct route. He demonstrated
a new method by writing an interpretation, a commentary that was the new thing itself.

The change which he introduced was not simply to
subordinate historical interpretation to "understand-

ing." It went far beyond that. It was basic to the historical method to eliminate the subjective element in the pursuit of objectivity, of "accuracy." It identified subjectivity as distortion. When it gradually became convinced that historians were inevitably prejudiced because of their own personal stance in their own world, it assumed that it could neutralize the historian's prejudice in selecting and arranging data by insisting that he frankly confess his personal prejudgments. Thus the reader would be able to remove the distortion which the historian's bias inevitably introduced.

For Barth the contrary was true. The subjectivity of the interpreter made a positive contribution to good interpretation. It was not to be eliminated as distortion. The interpreter needs, he said, to understand himself correctly. If he does, and is seriously concerned with serious questions, he will ask the questions the Bible asks. What was serious then is still serious today; so the interpreter should be concerned to ask the right questions, to make sure that his concern is with the ultimate. This will keep him from overlooking the ultimate concern of the book he is interpreting.

Barth's insistence upon the continuing nature of the spirit of the Bible looks two ways. It is not concerned with establishing contemporary meaning only. It is equally concerned to establish an understanding of the past in its own right. Thus he rejected Harnack's insistence that the interpreter's task was to get intellectual control of the object and insisted he must

remember that the object of his study was first subject, and must become so again and again.

Barth felt that the material superiority of Paul and
Luther to most moderns was so great that he must
take their basic approach seriously as a possibly valid
approach. Thus while he insisted upon our duty to
think in our own time and for our own time, his theology was rapidly identified as "neo-orthodoxy," as
Paulinism, as a rebirth of Lutheran Reformation theology. It brings theology to the interpretation of the
Bible, not apologetically, but as a valuable tool.

The generalizations presented in the opening sections of this chapter are made possible by the results
of Barth's work. They indicate the direct influence of
his work upon large numbers of interpreters.

RUDOLF BULTMANN

But not the least important influence of Barth was
his influence upon a single individual, Bultmann.
Bultmann recognized the second edition of Barth's
Romans as an attempt to express in language the
awareness of the distinctiveness and absoluteness of
religion, and he ranked it with Schleiermacher, Otto,
and Romans itself in this respect. Bultmann insisted
that Paul himself sometimes gave inadequate expression to this normative subject matter, and criticized
Barth for failing to recognize this limitation in Paul.

This limitation was most clearly recognized by
Bultmann in the mythical language of Paul. Yet the
limitation is substantial as well as linguistic, for the
subject matter of the myth is seen as inconsistent

with the subject matter that dominates the text. His objection was not alone to the objectifying and hence probably misleading language of myth. The language of apocalypticism (the picture of the sudden end of the world) with its dragons, angels, and deceiving demons is not, said Bultmann, saying anything about my existence, about the reality in which alone I could hear God. His insistence that theological statements spring from the believer's understanding and may therefore be more or less appropriate goes radically beyond Barth's position. This clears the way for the demythologizing of stuff as well as language.

DEMYTHOLOGIZATION

This $64 word labels the method of interpretation identified with Bultmann and his followers. The emphasis upon decoding the myth is an asset in distinguishing demythologization from liberalism's elimination of the incredible from the Bible. Yet the restatement in existentialist interpretation does also eliminate inadequate mythical concepts and the theological biblical statements that rested on them or sprang from them. Bultmann recognized that myths bear meaning that lies behind the uncongenial language, from which that meaning must be freed by reconstruction in existentialist terms. In an age in which everything good is given the adjective "depth," Bultmann's method could be called "depth interpretation." It delves below the surface of language and concepts to analyze basic concerns and basic phenomena, rather than to identify the "position" of the author. It then proceeds to interpret these basics in and to the contemporary world. Bultmannians speak of "precious kernel" and "foreign husk."

Myth, says Bultmann, intends to express the way man understands himself in his world, and should, therefore, be interpreted existentially. Myth expresses the faith that the known and controllable world has its ground and limit outside the known and controllable. Myth knows that man is dependent on the powers ruling beyond the known, and that in this dependency he can become free. But the myth's objectifying statements (inevitable and natural as they are) inevitably restrict and obscure its effectiveness in speaking of a power beyond. Thus Bultmann's method moves away from language (of which mythological language is the egregious example) back to a prior and more authentic understanding.

Applied to the New Testament this method locates Jesus in the historical environment of primitive Christianity. It identifies Paul and John as the normative core of that Christianity, John representing the peak because of the degree of its own demythologization of Jesus. Bornkamm's comment that this method "dehistoricizes" Jesus is relevant.

Bultmann has a theological-philosophical position. He has stated it in his *Theology of the New Testament.* I present it here in a summary from a review by Robinson in *Theology Today* (July, 1956).

"Johannine theology is presented in formal parallelism to Pauline theology in spite of considerable differences in vocabulary and theological topics.

Therefore a parallel summary of the two theologies will give the main line of Bultmann's Johannine Theology in terms familiar to the readers of Volume I, and will also outline Bultmann's nearest approach to a presentation of his own 'systematic theology.' A first section on 'Johannine Dualism' corresponds to the Pauline section on 'Man prior to the Revelation of Faith.' Instead of the Pauline anthropological terms 'body,' 'soul', 'spirit,' etc., it is now the Johannine use of Gnostic dualism and determinism which provides the material for an ontological analysis of man, revealing the historicity of human existence. This is followed by an analysis of man's factual ('ontic') status of non-authenticity, which Paul designates as living according to the flesh and John as 'the perversion of the creation into the "world." ' These analyses thus disclose the *Vorverständnis* (preliminary understanding) which a person has, if he is to be put into existential decision by the kerygma. With this preparation, the kerygma is next presented, in Pauline terms as the righteousness of God and his grace, and in Johannine terms as 'the "krisis" of the world.' All of Paul's terminologies for describing the saving event have been classified historically and shown to be inadequate attempts to express his faith, whereupon the normative question became the origin of his faith, and this was found in the presence of the saving-event in the proclaimed word. Similarly in the case of John, the language of the Gnostic myth is superseded, all of Jesus' person and work is summarized in him as the Word, and this Word is then identified with the preached word, in which one believed. This procedure is in each case (I, 300–302; II, 71) in the interest of uniting two meanings of faith into one act: acceptance of the facts of the kerygma and of their saving significance; and surrender of self and commitment to the reality of God's care. This is a typical instance of Bultmann's primary concern for maintaining in dialectic relationship the historical and the supra-historical—and also the justification for the immanent criticism that he continues one-sidedly the reaction against the 'historicism' of the nineteenth century by leaning heavily in the direction of the supra-historical.

"Since John does not expound *what* the revelation reveals about God, but only *that* the historical person Jesus reveals God, the only way to discuss further the revelation is to analyze the faith in which it is reflected. One is prepared for this final section of the outline, even apart from its specific Johannine justification, since the presentation of Pauline theology had moved to the same climax. Furthermore the Epilogue to Volume II contains a methodological and historical appendix designed to explain that theological statements are not the object of faith, but explications of the act of faith, so that their correct interpretation is to use them to define faith as the believer's new self-understanding."

POST-BULTMANN

The interpretation of the Bible in what has been called a post-Bultmannian period is varied in methodology. Two movements identify themselves as "New": The New Quest of the Historical Jesus, and the New Hermeneutic. Others continue to use methods that preceded Bultmann, methods which, in some cases, Bultmann did not discard but did either de-emphasize or reform.

The New Quest argues for the theological possibility and desirability of reopening the study of the historical Jesus. It sees significant overlapping between the historical Jesus and the content of the primitive preaching, the kerygma. It recognizes the importance of studying Jesus' understanding of existence, that understanding of existence which emerges in history from his words and deeds. This quest reintroduces a wide range of human experience which demythologization tended to read out of the canon, and thus brings the student closer to confronting that reality to which man responded in the past.

That the Quest is "New" has been denied by some scholars, that it is desirable has been denied by others. The debate has been lively, and has been welcomed by many as movement toward a restoration of balance in biblical interpretation. The leaders of the Quest are themselves moving toward a more systematically inclusive method: the New Hermeneutic.

The New Hermeneutic embraces the whole theological enterprise as a movement of language. It begins with the language of the Word of God in Scripture, a language which is itself in one sense a translation of that Word. It goes on to the language of the Bible in a modern contemporary idiom, another translation. And it proceeds to the theologically based sermon preached today, in which God speaks again. This new interpretation cannot be limited to exegesis, a subdivision of biblical study. On the contrary it becomes coterminous with Christian theology as the statement of the meaning of Scripture for our day.

This method emphasizes the interpretive interrelatedness of language, translation, and exegesis. In some of its early formulations it indicates that it runs the risk of becoming a new pedantic scholasticism, irrelevant to our experience. But it also contains the promise of producing a theologically based understanding of Scripture more rigorous, more comprehensive, and more relevant than its predecessors.

At the same time archeological studies continue. Literary criticism enriches understanding of Scripture. Sociological history, though badly wounded, has not expired, and is valuable as a counterbalance to abstractions gone to extremes. The bibliography to this chapter illustrates the continued activity of scholarship in these areas. The historians cited there do not aim at an impossibly complete objectivity. They do insist on the objective reality of the past, and that their results must be objective enough to stand up under the criticism of their peers. They admit that their knowledge is a knowledge of probability, but they insist that it is not, therefore, improbable. They are interested in "bare" facts only as these contribute to their knowledge of contemporary human understanding of these facts.

In the last quarter-century, study of the Bible has been greatly stimulated by three sensational discoveries. In each case what was discovered was, in effect, an ancient library: the Dead Sea Scrolls, the Gnostic Documents from Nag Hammadi, and the Bodmer Papyri.

The Dead Sea Scrolls are the books of a Palestinian Jewish sect. They were found in caves near the shores of the Dead Sea. They date from somewhere between the second century B.C. and the second century A.D. They contain Hebrew copies of much of our Old Testament, the most extensive being Isaiah and a commentary on Habakkuk, and parts of all the books of our Protestant Old Testament except Esther. These documents are older by five or six centuries than previously available extensive Hebrew copies. Thus our ability to validate the wording of the Hebrew Bible is greatly increased.

But the scrolls have an additional value. In such scrolls as the Manual of Discipline and others, we get an insight into a sectarian group in the Judaism of Jesus' day. Whether or not this group is identical with the group called the Essenes in other sources, the scrolls illuminate formerly shadowy areas of Palestinian life. Early journalistic hopes that the scrolls would "explain" Jesus and primitive Christianity have evaporated, or been moderated. For the scrolls make a larger contribution to our knowledge of Judaism than to our knowledge of Christianity. They make a larger contribution to our understanding of Acts than to our understanding of the Gospels. But they do clear up many a detail formerly obscure. And, not least in importance, they present a clear picture of one of the many religious strands that existed in the vigorous life of Judaism at the beginning of the Christian era. They reveal a fanatical sect, strict in their legalism, consciously expecting God to end the wicked age in which they lived, and withdrawn from that wickedness.

From Nag Hammadi another library is slowly being published. It is a Christian library, but a library whose Christianity today is identified as heretical. Its heresy is called Gnosticism, a vague term with broad meanings. It is characterized by a dualism with two worlds, by revealed "knowledge" of the origin and nature of these worlds and of man's predicament in this world and his way out. These books were probably composed in the second century A.D.; the copies found were written in Coptic in approximately the fourth century A.D. They include a Gospel of Thomas (sayings of Jesus, no actions), a Gospel of Truth (no sayings or deeds of Jesus, only his meaning), an Apocryphon of John, and others yet to be published. They may reflect an important and substantial segment of primitive Egyptian Christianity.

The Bodmer Papyri are Christian documents in Greek and Coptic. The actual copies range in date from about A.D. 200 to the fourth or fifth century or even to the ninth century A.D. They include a copy of the Gospel of John (P 66) from about A.D. 200, and an equally ancient copy of much of Luke and John (P 75). Other books of the Bible in this library are, from the third century, Jude, I and II Peter, III Corinthians; from the fourth century, Proverbs in Coptic, John and Gen. 1:1–4:2 in Bohairic, Exod. 1:1–15:21 in Sahidic, Deut. 1:1–10:7 in Sahidic, Matt. 14:28–28:20 and Rom. 1:1–2:3; and from the sixth or seventh century, Acts and fragments of James, Peter, John, and Jude.

These documents have notably advanced our understanding of the transmission of the Scriptures in Greek and Coptic. They give us older and valuable copies of non-biblical literature from primitive Christian times. Their major contribution to biblical study lies in the realm of what used to be called "lower criticism," the establishment of an accurately worded edition of the Greek New Testament. Here their contribution has already been sensational, and much of their significance awaits further study.

BIBLIOGRAPHY ON RECENT INTERPRETATION AND DISCOVERY

BRAATEN, C. E., and HARRISVILLE, R. A. (eds.). *Kerygma and History: A Symposium on the Theology of Rudolf Bultmann.* Nashville: Abingdon, 1962.

————. *The Historical Jesus and the Kerygmatic Christ: Essays on the New Quest of the Historical Jesus.* Nashville: Abingdon, 1964.
These two volumes give a good cross-section of essays.

Fuller, R. H. *The New Testament in Current Study*. New York: Scribner's, 1962.

A series of lectures, popular style, covers two decades.

Von Rad, Gerhard. *Old Testament Theology* (trans. by D. M. G. Stalker). New York: Harper & Bros., 1962.

Rowley, H. H. *The Old Testament and Modern Study*. Oxford: Clarendon Press, 1951.

Zahrnt, Heinz. *The Historical Jesus*. New York: Harper & Row, 1963.

A readable survey of study from Reimarus to Bornkamm.

Robinson, J. M. *A New Quest of the Historical Jesus*. Naperville: Allenson, 1959.

A statement by one of the leaders of the "New Quest."

Robinson, J. M., and Cobb, J. B., Jr. (eds.). *The New Hermeneutic (New Frontiers in Theology: Discussions among Continental and American Theologians*, Vol. II). New York: Harper & Row, 1964.

Grant, R. M. *A Historical Introduction to the New Testament*. New York: Harper & Row, 1963.

A comprehensive introduction to all aspects of New Testament study. A stimulating review of methods and results.

Gottwald, N. K. *A Light to the Nations*. New York: Harper & Bros., 1959.

A good general introduction to the interpretation of the Old Testament.

Wright, G. E. *Biblical Archeology* (rev. ed.). Philadelphia: Westminster, 1962.

Bright, John. *A History of Israel*. Philadelphia: Westminster, 1959.

Pfeiffer, R. H. *Introduction to the Old Testament*. New York: Harper & Bros., 1948.

A scholarly introduction to the literature of the Old Testament.

Westermann, C. (ed.). *Essays on Old Testament Hermeneutics*. Richmond: John Knox Press, 1963.

BORNKAMM, G. *Jesus of Nazareth* (trans. by IRENE and FRASER McLUSKEY with JAMES M. ROBINSON). New York: Harper & Row, 1960.
The best contemporary treatment of the subject from Germany.

BULTMANN, R. *Theology of the New Testament* (trans. by KENDRICK GROBEL). New York: Scribner's, 1951–55.
This is the central item in English translation of Bultmann's work.

JEREMIAS, J. *The Parables of Jesus.* New York: Scribner's, 1955.

KNOX, J. *Jesus, Lord and Christ.* New York: Harper & Bros., 1958.
Stimulating study of the interaction of faith and history.

SECULAR HISTORICAL METHOD

POWICKE, F. M. *History, Freedom and Religion.* London: Oxford University Press, *ca.* 1940.

———. *Three Lectures Given in the Hall of Balliol College, Oxford.* London: Oxford University Press, 1947.

COLLINGWOOD, R. G. *The Idea of History.* Oxford: Clarendon Press, 1946.

BLOCH, MARC. *The Historian's Craft.* New York: Knopf, 1953.
The insights of a great historian into methodology. Unsurpassed.

BUTTERFIELD, H. *Christianity and History.* London: Bell, 1950.

THE DEAD SEA SCROLLS

CROSS, F. M., JR. *The Ancient Library of Qumran.* Garden City, N.Y.: Doubleday, 1958.

GASTER, T. H. *The Dead Sea Scriptures in English Translation with Introduction and Notes.* Garden City, N.Y.: Doubleday, 1956.

BROWNLEE, W. H. *The Meaning of the Qumran Scrolls for the Bible.* New York: Oxford University Press, 1964.
Although this work gives special attention to the Isaiah Scroll, it covers all aspects of study of the scrolls, and has extensive bibliographical footnotes.

THE BEATTY PAPYRI

KENYON, F. G. *The Chester Beatty Biblical Papyri: Descriptions and Texts of Twelve Manuscripts on Papyrus of the Greek Bible.* London: Emery Walker, 1933.

THE BODMER PAPYRI

Published by various scholars (V. MARTIN, M. TESTUZ, *et al.*), entitled *Papyrus Bodmer I, II*, etc. Cologne and Geneva: Bibliothèque Bodmer, 1956———.

NAG HAMMADI DOCUMENTS

DORESSE, J. *The Secret Books of the Egyptian Gnostics* (trans. by PHILIP MAIRET). London: Hollis & Carter, 1960.

Doresse regards Gnosticism as pre-Christian. His survey of some of these documents was inevitably hurried.

GROBEL, K. *The Gospel of Truth: A Valentinian Meditation on the Gospel: Translation and Commentary.* London: A. & C. Black, 1960.

GUILLAUMONT, A., PUECH, H.-CH., QUISPEL, G., TILL, W., and YASSAH 'ABD AL MASIH. *The Gospel According to Thomas: Coptic Text Established and Translated.* New York: Harper & Bros., 1959.

WILSON, R. McL. *The Gospel of Philip. Translated from the Coptic Text, with an Introduction and Commentary.* London: Mowbray, 1962.

The Introduction is valuable for its judicious appraisal of the place of all three gospels within Gnosticism, and of the origin of Gnosticism. Wilson recognizes the possibility that Gnosticism may be the result of Christianity's impact on its world.

General Bibliography

The student's attention is drawn to the presence of the special bibliographies at the end of the chapters. In those lists will be found introduction to the literature on canon, text, translation, and interpretation. An attempt was made there to include books that would introduce the reader to further literature on the subject. This is supplemented by listing here some of the periodicals, dictionaries, and commentaries that will lead the student into broader areas and make it possible for him to keep abreast of recent developments.

Of the special works on bibliography itself, the student will find the following helpful: S. J. Case, J. T. McNeill, W. W. Sweet, W. Pauck, and M. Spinka, *A Bibliographical Guide to the History of Christianity* (Chicago: University of Chicago Press, 1931).

Five of the leading periodicals which deal with the study of the Bible are the *Journal of Biblical Literature and Exegesis, New Testament Studies, Revue biblique, Zeitschrift für die neutestamentliche Wissenschaft,* and *Zeitschrift für die alttestamentliche Wissenschaft.*

More general in scope of subjects treated, but valuable in the presentation of significant studies of the Bible are the *Journal of Religion,* the *Anglican Theological Review,* the *Journal of Theological Studies,* the *Harvard Theological Review, Church History,* and the *American Journal of Semitic Languages and Literatures.* The book-review sections of the journals listed in this paragraph are of value in keeping the student informed about new works; this is especially true of the *Journal of Theological Studies.* The *Harvard Theological Review* has no book-review section but, like most of the others listed here, occasionally publishes lengthy surveys of recent study in some one area. For current information in the general field of archeology, see the *American Journal of Archaeology,* the *Bulletin* and *Annual* of the American Schools of Oriental Research, the Palestine Exploration Fund Quarterly Statement.

In the field of dictionaries, two old publications are of great value: the eleventh (twelfth or thirteenth) edition of the *Encyclopaedia Britannica* (1912) for solid factual studies as of that date;

and the five-volume *Dictionary of the Bible* (1898–1904) of J. Hastings. Similar to the Hastings work is the *Encyclopaedia biblica* edited by T. K. Cheyne and A. S. Black in four volumes (1899–1903). Similar in size and solid value to the *Britannica* is the exhaustive study of Christian archeology edited by Cabrol, *Dictionnaire d'archéologie chrétienne et de liturgie*, which is still in process of publication. *The Interpreter's Dictionary of the Bible* (New York: Abingdon, 1962); *The New Schaff-Herzog Encyclopedia of Religious Knowledge* (13 vols.; Grand Rapids, Mich.: Baker Book House, 1951; reprint based on 3d ed., New York: Funk and Wagnalls, 1908–14); the *Twentieth Century Encyclopedia of Religious Knowledge* (an extension of *The New Schaff-Herzog Encyclopedia of Religious Knowledge* (2 vols.; Grand Rapids: Baker Book House, 1955); and Hastings' *Dictionary of the Bible* (rev. ed. by F. C. Grant and H. H. Rowley; New York: Scribner, 1963) are useful collections of scholarly lore.

The student has probably already discovered for himself that the separate volumes of the great commentary series are not of uniform quality. The general evaluations given here are not, therefore, equally applicable to all the works in any series. The outstanding technical series in English is still the *International Critical Commentary on the Holy Scriptures of the Old and New Testaments*, edited by Driver, Plummer, and Briggs. At the intermediate level there is little to choose between *The New Century Bible*, edited by W. F. Adeney for the Oxford University Press, and *The Cambridge Bible for Schools and Colleges*, edited in the Old Testament by A. F. Kirkpatrick and in the New Testament by R. St. John Parry, for the Cambridge University Press. Both of these have now passed middle age. In German the *Handbuch zum Neuen Testament*, edited by Lietzmann, and the *Handbuch zum Alten Testament*, edited by O. Eissfeldt, are the most stimulating and up-to-date series. *The Interpreter's Bible* (New York: Abingdon, 1952) is the best of recent popular commentaries.

The student's attention is called to the one-volume commentaries; e.g. *The Twentieth Century Bible Commentary* (rev. ed. by G. H. Davies, A. Richardson, and C. L. Wallis; New York: Harper & Bros., 1955); *Peake's Commentary on the Bible* (general editor and New Testament editor: Matthew Black; Old Testament editor: H. H. Rowley; New York: Nelson, 1962); and *The Interpreter's One Volume Commentary on the Bible* (ed. by Charles M. Laymon; New York: Abingdon Press, 1964).

Index of Authors and Subjects

✣

Index of Passages Cited

✼